"Father John Jay Hughes has led an extraordinary life at the intersection of many of the great Christian controversies of our time. His steady defense of the conviction that led him into full communion with the Catholic Church—that the truth Catholicism bears is not a truth for Catholics only, but *the* truth of the human condition—is both a testimony to grace and to his own personal and intellectual courage. Young people looking for a winsome introduction to the debates that produced the Catholic Church of the twenty-first century will find Father Hughes a friendly guide to the immediate past. Those of us a little further along will recognize in his autobiographical reflections many shared adventures—and come away from that recognition with a fresh insight into our own experience."

George Weigel
Senior Fellow, Ethics and Public Policy Center, Washington
Author of *Witness to Hope: The Biography of Pope John Paul II*

"John Jay Hughes offers the most profound memoir of a personal spiritual search since Thomas Merton's *Seven Storey Mountain* more than half a century ago. As a descendant of John Jay, Father Hughes' roots are as deep and Protestant as those of America itself. He moves out of the shadows of that great tradition, becoming a Catholic and later a priest at the high cost of estrangement from his father. We are all enriched by these gentle, beautifully written recollections of great faith, enormous courage, and good sense that reveal his love for life as well as his gentle concern for all that is human. Shortly into the book you will wish that you knew the author and by the time you finish you will happily feel that you do."

Eugene Kennedy, PhD
Emeritus Professor of Psychology,
Loyola University of Chicago

"Father John Jay Hughes is one of the most learned and gentle priests in the United States, and he preaches marvelous, short, and meaty sermons of considerable literary quality. Father Hughes has lived a fascinating life, some of it as an ocean sailor during adventurous vacations. He springs from a devout Anglican family and became a Roman Catholic at a young age and in a very thoughtful, reflective way. No one today writes as well as he about the beauty of the vocation of living as a Catholic priest. His autobiography is an engrossing, inspiring read."

Michael Novak
George Frederick Jewett Chair in Religion and Public Policy
American Enterprise Institute
Winner, Templeton Prize for Progress in Religion, 1994

"With his gift for the telling example, John Jay Hughes has attracted a wide circle of admirers for essays that link universal themes to everyday life. Now, in this fascinating memoir, he recounts his own journey through life in a way that illuminates the perennial dilemmas that all men and women face. Readers of all faiths will find their own struggles illuminated in this graceful and wise narrative."

Mary Ann Glendon
Learned Hand Professor of Law, Harvard University
United States Ambassador to the Holy See

"John Jay Hughes is among the most distinguished and able writers in the English-speaking world. His memoirs, relating the moving story of his conversion, his Harvard education, and association as a student with Professor Joseph Ratzinger, should indeed find great interest in a wide audience."

The Most Reverend John R. Quinn
Archbishop Emeritus of San Francisco

Cardinal Newman, originally a Protestant from an evangelical family, wrote the story of his conversion to Catholicism in terms of his disenchantment with the via media of the Anglican Communion. John Jay Hughes, descendant of the founding father, John Jay, has written the story of his conversion in terms of the strain he underwent in separating from his father, also an Episcopal priest. The climax of the tale is the discovery after his father's death of an undelivered letter which in effect reunited the two men.

Justus George Lawler
Editor-at-Large, Continuum International Publishing Group.

"The story told by Father John Jay Hughes is a remarkable account of a life engaged by a wide experience of different Christian communities, as well as the many worlds of Catholicism, joined to theological and personal reflections that will undoubtedly be appreciated by many readers."

The Reverend Richard John Neuhaus
Editor-in-Chief, *First Things*

NO ORDINARY
FOOL

John Jay Hughes

No Ordinary Fool

A Testimony to Grace

Foreword by George Weigel

Tate Publishing & *Enterprises*

This title is also available as a Tate Out Loud product. Visit www.tatepublishing.com for more information.

Published by Tate Publishing & Enterprises, LLC
127 E. Trade Center Terrace | Mustang, Oklahoma 73064 USA
1.888.361.9473 | www.tatepublishing.com

Tate Publishing is committed to excellence in the publishing industry. The company reflects the philosophy established by the founders, based on Psalm 68:11,
"The Lord gave the word and great was the company of those who published it."

Cover design by Isaiah McKee
Interior design by Stefanie Rooney
Cover photo: The author greets his old teacher in Münster, Joseph Ratzinger, now Pope Benedict XVI, in Rome on March 3, 2007. Photo by permission of Osservatore Romano.

Published in the United States of America

ISBN: 978-1-60604-182-6
1. Biography & Autobiography
2. Religous
08.05.14

Also by John Jay Hughes

Absolutely Null and Utterly Void: The Papal Condemnation of Anglican Orders, 1896

Stewards of the Lord: A Reappraisal of Anglican Orders

Man for Others: Reflections on Christian Priesthood

Der priesterliche Dienst VI

Zur Frage der anglikanischen Weihen

(Quaestiones disputatae 59*)*

Proclaiming the Good News:

Homilies for the "A" Cycle

Homilies for the "B" Cycle

Homilies for the "C" Cycle

Sea Psalms

Pontiffs: Popes who Shaped History

Stories Jesus Told: Modern Meditations on the Parables

For my beloved parents
who gave me so much,
and for Bina,
who made us a family again.

Table of Contents

Foreword

Luke 12:53—Christ's stern statement that he had come to set "father against son and son against father, mother against daughter and daughter against her mother, mother-in-law against her daughter-in-law and daughter-in-law against her mother-in-law"—is a text frequently swept under the homiletic carpet, the preacher perhaps suggesting that Jesus was having a bit of a bad day. The text is indeed a challenging one; no one could ever say that Jesus lacked edge. Yet it is also true that the Lord was not commanding us to despise our closest relatives for his sake. Rather, the point of Luke 12:53 is that allegiance to Christ puts every human bond of affection and intimacy into a new light—the light of grace. The all-demanding and all-consuming love of the God Who is Love shapes and reshapes all the other loves of our lives, and indeed directs those human loves toward their proper end. That can be a difficult process at times. But it is, ultimately, a redemptive process. Encountering that love and being transformed by it is how we realize our human destiny.

Christ is not, in other words, a family wrecker.

But sometimes, in the drama of the Christian life, it can happen: allegiance to Christ can attenuate, even sever (temporarily, one hopes), the bonds of human love. Fathers and sons, mothers and daughters, brothers and sisters can come to grief because of the love of Christ and because of what Christ demands. It is, perhaps, a rare circumstance these days. But its rarity only underscores its drama.

Father John Jay Hughes has led a most dramatic life, his journey of faith and priestly ministry taking him into the swirling center of many a theological, ecclesiastical, and ecumenical controversy in the second half of the twentieth century. Father Hughes has lived the drama of the Catholic Church in the modern world in a unique way, and some of the scars show; it is a sign of his gratitude before the immense power of God's grace that he lets them show. What gives Father Hughes' story a distinctive personal power, however, is the price he was required to pay for following the call of conscience and conviction into the Catholic Church and out of the Episcopal Church—a Christian community into whose clerical family he had been born and raised, a Christian community in which he had been baptized, confirmed, and ordained. That passage from Canterbury to Rome cost him dearly, for it severely weakened his relationship to the father he loved and admired, himself an Episcopal clergyman. I won't spoil the story by going into its dramatic details here. Suffice it to say that John Jay Hughes—direct descendant of one of America's Founding Fathers and a certified member of whatever aristocracy exists in these United States—knows in his bones what Jesus was talking about in Luke 12:53.

No Ordinary Fool is also an invitation to explore worlds long gone: the upper-crust world of New York Anglicanism when it was as close to an established Church as anything can be in America; the world of mid-twentieth-century German theological scholarship, full of the conviction that classic Christian truth claims and post-Kantian modern intellectual life can and must be reconciled; the world of the Second Vatican Council, now receding fast in the ecclesiastical rearview mirror; the world of immediate post-Vatican II Catholicism, full of energy and not so full of sense. Father Hughes' story is the story of a precocious boy growing up in a culture skeptical of refined things and given to celebrating ordinariness; the story of an American trying to fit himself into the sometimes insular world of the German academy; the story of an Anglo-Catholic trying to find his priestly way in a Church dominated by Irish-Americans; the story of a theologian and historian at work in an American Catholicism that has never taken either theology or its own history seriously. If this suggests that Father Hughes did not enjoy a smooth "career path," as the management types say, well, the suggestion is appropriate. But the life story told here is all the more interesting for its cragginess and edges.

Above all, this is the story of a man who, from his twelfth birthday, believed himself called to be a priest of Jesus Christ, and who was willing to sacrifice quite literally everything toward that call. At a moment in American Catholic history when whatever attention the mass media pays to the Catholic priesthood is given to the rotten apples in the clerical barrel, John Jay Hughes' autobiography is a welcome reminder that there have been, and are, tens of thousands of accomplished, dedicated, and holy men in America who have given up much of what the world values in order to be priests of Jesus Christ. Jay Hughes' personal story is such that he is, in truth, a singularity in the galaxy of the American priesthood. But his love for his priesthood and his dedication to it form an even deeper bond with his brother priests, and with his fellow Catholics, than any of the more conventional bonds. For it is a bond forged in the sometimes harsh and dreadful love of the Christ of Luke 12:53.

Enjoy the story, for it's a good one. At the same time, however, ponder the meaning of the life of Father John Jay Hughes: a life given to the truth of God, revealed in Christ, and made available to us in the Church. The greatest of human lives is a life lived in fidelity to the truth that sets us free in the deepest meaning of human freedom. That is why Father Hughes' life is a great one and why I, with many others, wish him *ad multos annos* (many more years) as he shares the story of his life with the Church and the world.

George Weigel

Distinguished Senior Fellow of the Ethics and
Public Policy Center in Washington

Catholic theologian and the author of many books,
including the *New York Times* bestseller, *Witness
to Hope: The Biography of Pope John Paul II.*

Author's Introduction

When the late Cardinal Heenan of Westminster published his autobiography in two volumes (an indulgence not granted to the lower clergy), he called the first installment, *Not the Whole Truth.*[1] I might have used the title myself, had it not been preempted by an author more eminent than myself. The title I have chosen instead is explained at the end of chapter two.

Biographers and autobiographers alike face the same problem: what to include and what to leave out. There is a case for reticence, within limits. As they say in the theater, "Send the audience home wanting more." And Chesterton enjoins reticence when he writes: "No man dare say of himself, over his own name, how badly he has behaved. No man dare say of himself, over his own name, how well he has behaved."

Moreover, a too detailed account can become so tedious that it will not be read. That was the case (though I was unable to recognize this at the time) with my first attempt to tell my story. Written twelve years ago, it was almost twice the length of this book. Unsurprisingly, it was turned down by more than twenty publishers, on both sides of the Atlantic.

Why tell one's story at all? The reasons for writing are as varied as the writers. My own motive is indicated in my subtitle. I wish to bear witness to the Lord's ability to write straight on the crooked lines of our unfaithfulness. Evangelical Protestants sometimes overdo personal testimony. Catholics too often fear it. Passages in the letters of St. Paul, and in St. Augustine's *Confessions*, show that personal witness, rightly handled, has unique power.

In telling my story, I have had the great advantage—in addition to the excellent memory given to me by a generous Creator—of possessing all the letters I wrote to my father. They came back to me after his death. I am grateful to two contemporaries at Kelham, Richard Rutt and Clifford Smart, for sharing with me their memories of the place, and correcting some details of mine. And I owe special thanks to my British publisher, Tom Longford, for encouraging me to resurrect a project which I thought permanently moribund.

Beyond that I am grateful to our heavenly friends, the saints, almost twenty in number, women and men alike, whose prayers I invoke daily. It has been my practice for many years always to pray for the guidance and inspiration of the Holy Spirit before any literary task, no matter how slight. The Spirit has never failed me. It is due to this divine assistance that I have yet to experience writer's block. And so I can say with the psalmist: *Non nobis, Domine, non nobis, sed nomine tuo da gloriam* ("Not unto us, O Lord, not unto us, but unto thy name be the praise").

I have shown myself as I was: mean and contemptible, good, high-minded and sublime ... I have unveiled my inmost self as Thou hast seen it, O Eternal Being. Gather round me the countless host of my fellow-men; let them hear my confessions, lament for my unworthiness, and blush for my imperfections. Then let each of them in turn reveal, with the same frankness, the secrets of his heart at the foot of the Throne, and say, if he dare, "I was better than that man!"

Jean-Jacques Rousseau, *Confessions*, Book I

What shall I render to the Lord, who recalls these things to my memory, but my soul feels no fear from the recollection? ... I attribute to your grace and mercy that you have melted my sins away like ice. I also attribute to your grace whatever evil acts I have not done.

St. Augustine, *Confessions* II, vii (15)

I

The Best Time to be a Priest

In 1970 a forty-three-year-old professor of Catholic theology in Germany wrote: "It seems certain to me that very hard times await the Church. Her crisis has hardly begun."[2] Today the author of those words is Pope Benedict XVI. What form the hard times he predicted would take, Joseph Ratzinger (as he then was) did not say. Today we know. The crisis of priestly sexual misconduct with minors, which burst upon Catholics in the United States in January 2002, is the most painful that we have ever experienced. Similar things have happened elsewhere.

If we hear less about them elsewhere, this is for two reasons. People in many places, the Latin countries in particular, are more keenly aware of something pointed out by retired Archbishop John R. Quinn of San Francisco at the height of the sexual abuse crisis: "We have to dispose of the illusion that there was a time in the past when these behaviors did not occur and that there will be some future time when these behaviors will cease to occur. As long as there is human nature these problems will occur, and they have always occurred."[3] The second reason is the United States legal system.

Because American tort law now gives lawyers up to half of the awards they obtain for their clients, the sums demanded of defendants have risen exponentially in recent decades. Over a decade ago a British friend told me that he had had to resign from Lloyds of London because of damage awards in American courts. The costs to the Catholic Church in the United States have been staggering.

The Church has been through the fires of adversity before. Each time it has emerged purified and renewed. The Protestant Reformation produced the renewed and disciplined Church of the Catholic Reform or Counter-Reformation, with the Jesuits in the vanguard. From the fierce persecution of Catholics in the French Revolution came numerous new religious orders for men and women and dynamic missionary outreach in Africa and Asia.

It was this recurrent pattern of renewal through suffering which caused Cardinal Ratzinger to tell the German journalist Peter Seewald in 1996: "The Church needs a revolution of faith ... It must part with its goods, in order to preserve its treasure."[4] He was talking not about earthly but heavenly treasure, the Good News of the Gospel: that God loves sinners; that his love for us is a free gift, bestowed on us not because we are good enough, but because he is so good that he longs to share his love with us.

How are Catholic priests holding up under today's avalanche of bad publicity? Astonishingly well, according to surveys. Between September 2003 and April 2005, St. Luke's Institute in Silver Spring, Maryland, a treatment center for priests with psychological problems, questioned 1,286 priests at their annual convocations in sixteen American dioceses about their experience of priesthood. Asked to comment on the statement, "Overall, I am happy as a priest," over 90% agreed. More than 81% said they would choose priesthood again. Only 6% were thinking of leaving. What other profession could match those numbers?

How is that possible? Why would any man in his right mind want to be a Catholic priest today? In the article cited above regarding the sexual abuse crisis, Archbishop Quinn answers this question as follows: "I believe that this is the best time in the history of the Church to be a priest, because it is a time when there can be only one reason for being a priest or for remaining a priest—that is to 'be with' Christ. It is not for perks or applause or respect or position or money or any other worldly gain or advantage. Those things either no longer exist or are swiftly passing. The priest of today is forced to choose whether he wants to give himself to the real Christ, who embraced poverty, including the poverty of the commonplace, rejection, misrepresentation—the real Christ of the gospels—or whether, with the mistaken throngs of Jesus time, he wants an earthly, worldly messiah for whom success follows upon success."

The Chicago priest-sociologist Fr. Andrew Greeley writes, "Priests who like being priests are among the happiest men in the world."[5] Those words lifted me out of my chair when I read them. "Andy, you're right!" I e-mailed him, "I can confirm that from my own experience." In his 2004 book, *Priests: A Calling in Crisis*, Greeley writes that the real problem of priestly morale today is that priests, though happy themselves, think that other priests are not happy.

Are we priests indifferent to the failings of our brothers who have abused the young? I don't know a single priest who is not deeply saddened by the revelations of recent years. Some have said that they fear wearing clerical dress in public, lest they be vilified and scorned—the "rejection" mentioned by Archbishop Quinn, which links us with "the real Christ," himself rejected by those for whom he laid down his life.

Say, if you like, that I lead a sheltered life. But I have yet to encounter rejection. On the contrary, I have experienced love and support from those we priests were ordained to serve, far beyond anything we deserve. On Holy Thursday 2002, at the height of the sexual abuse crisis, St. Louis priests gathered for the Chrism Mass at which priests the world over renew our priestly commitment and the bishop consecrates the Holy Oils to be used in the ensuing year for baptism, confirmation, holy orders, and the anointing of the sick. As we walked in procession, more than two hundred strong, into our cathedral, we passed through ranks of applauding laypeople holding signs which said: "We support our priests" and "We love our priests." Did we deserve that outpouring of love and support? We knew we did not. But we were grateful nonetheless. I cannot have been the only priest whose eyes were moist.

No vocation brings uninterrupted joy. Every life is shadowed by the Cross. A widow spoke for married people when she told me, "Father, when you walk up to the altar on your wedding day, you don't see the Stations of the Cross."[6] If priesthood, like marriage, leads to Calvary, it leads beyond Calvary to resurrection—and unending joy.

There is, first, the joy of preaching the Gospel: feeding God's people from the table of his Word. An evangelical hymn defines the teacher's task thus: "Tell me the old, old, story /

Of Jesus and his love." John's Gospel says it more briefly, in words once posted inside pulpits for the preacher to see: "Sir, we would like to see Jesus" (John 12:21). His story, and Jesus' words, uphold us when we are down, rebuke us when we go astray, and fill our mouths with laughter and our tongues with joy (to use the psalmist's words) when the sunshine of God's love shines upon us.

There is also the joy of pastoral ministry. Like priests everywhere, I have witnessed miracles of God's grace in the people we serve. Not ten years ago a man came into my confessional bruised and bloodied from a failed marriage. Then one of our CEO Catholics (Christmas and Easter only), he is today a daily communicant and a frequent penitent. Every priest has stories like that, many of them more dramatic.

What nourishes me most, however—next to the daily half hour I spend waiting on God in silence before Mass—is the privilege, so far beyond any man's deserving, of celebrating Mass and feeding God's holy people with the Bread of Life. It was that which drew me to priesthood when I was not yet in my teens. Every time I served Mass, I thought: *One day I'll stand there. I'll wear those vestments. I'll say those words.*

As a Catholic priest, I have experienced the joy of celebrating Mass all over the world: in tiny chapels and great cathedrals; in hotel rooms in China and Vietnam; on little Rottnest Island off Australia's west coast; at Mother Teresa's tomb in Calcutta; on ships at sea, from small sailing vessels to 2,000-passenger cruise ships; in St. Mark's Cathedral in Venice and at Notre Dame in Paris, where I was asked to offer prayers in German and English for the hordes of tourists who often outnumber the local worshipers. Everywhere the welcome has been the same, from brother priests to laypeople of all ages and both sexes, whose devotion and faith inspire us priests and often put us to shame.

Writing in April 2005 to my old teacher in Münster, Germany, Joseph Ratzinger, to express my delight at his election as pope and assure him of my prayers, I closed the letter, "In the joy of our common priesthood." What more can one say than that? From age twelve, priesthood has been all I ever wanted. If I were to die tonight, I would die a happy man.

2

"All Daddy's Friends are Fools."

My earliest memory is being scared of sheep. They were in a field between the vicarage and parish church at Ullenhall, an English village some fifteen miles south of Birmingham. It was the summer of 1931. My Anglophile father, with two degrees from Oxford and since 1927 headmaster of the Cathedral Choir School and Precentor at the Cathedral of St. John the Divine in New York City, was supplying for the Ullenhall vicar during the latter's extended summer holiday.

Having just passed my third birthday in May, I was far smaller than a large sheep. The assurances of my parents that the animals were more afraid of me than I was of them carried no conviction.

Equally unconvincing were my father's assurances that I would not get wet on the daily bicycle rides he and my mother took me on that summer. I rode in a basket fixed to the handlebars of one of the bicycles. I protested each time, pointing out that it was bound to rain and that when it did I would get wet.

"Fiddledy-dee, child," my father would reply. "It won't rain."

Despite these assurances, a folded mackintosh (the first word I learned for a raincoat) was invariably placed beneath me in the basket. This was put on me when it rained—which it always did. The rain trickled down my neck. I hated it.

* * *

I had, I now realize, a magical childhood. My mother, Marguerite Montgomery Jay ("Peggy"), bore me as her first child on May 14, 1928, at the Sloane Hospital for Women in Manhattan. Two more children followed: my sister, Jane, in 1930, my brother, Dudley, in 1932. Through my mother, I am a seventh-generation direct descendant of John Jay, one of our nation's Founding Fathers and its first Chief Justice.

My father, William Dudley Foulke Hughes, was a priest in the Episcopal Church and himself the son of an Anglican priest, Stanley Carnaghan Hughes, for thirty-five years Rector of Trinity Church in Newport, Rhode Island, a beautiful colonial structure with a soaring steeple built in 1726 to a design by Sir Christopher Wren, who had died three years previously in London. This grandfather was always known in the family as "Akn" (rhymes with "rockin"), supposedly the first attempt of his eldest son, my father, to say "father." Akn died in 1944 and lies buried in the churchyard of Trinity Church, next to his wife Lydia Foulke (who died of leukemia two years before I was born) under a massive flat stone with the Latin inscription: *Ecce sacerdos qui in diebus suis Deo placuit et inventus justus* ("Behold a priest who in his days pleased God and was found righteous.")

Akn was the son of a Presbyterian minister and had served briefly in the ministry of that Church himself before deciding to become an Anglican priest. In six generations the Hughes family contributed some thirty ministers to the Presbyterian Church. One of them, the Reverend James H. Hughes, who died in 1821, was the founder of Miami University in Oxford, Ohio.

My Hughes ancestors, like the Foulkes (the family of my paternal grandmother), were not Irish (as American Catholics always assume), but Welsh—the Irish who couldn't swim. The Jays and the Soleliacs (the family of my maternal grandmother) were French Huguenots. I believe myself to be the first Catholic in my family since the Reformation—and because of my descent from the first Chief Justice, one of the few Americans to appear both in the *Social Register* and the *Official Catholic Directory.*

Four of my great-grandparents were living at the time of my birth. I clearly recall the two great-grandmothers. One of them, Mary Taylor Reeves of Cincinnati, was married to William Dudley Foulke, a lawyer and prosperous Quaker from Richmond, Indiana. A crusader for civil service reform and women's suffrage, he was appointed by his friend, President Theodore Roosevelt, to the United States Civil Service Commission in 1901. The author of a shelf full of books (in a day when publication was easier than it is today), he tells in his *Hoosier Autobiography* of his father's explanation of investing, imparted to him during a walk on his twenty-first birthday.

"I buy these securities when they are cheap," he told his son William. "I sell them when they are expensive."

I have yet to encounter sounder financial advice.

Do all children love their grandparents? I certainly loved mine. Akn lived in a beautiful house with a million-dollar view of the entrance to Newport harbor from the back terrace. As a schoolmaster, my father enjoyed a three months' summer vacation. In my early years, part of this would be spent with my paternal grandfather in Newport. With Jane and Dudley I enjoyed some of the happiest days of an idyllic childhood there. Sometimes we were joined by our double cousins, Arthur and Sally, the children of my father's brother and my mother's sister. The two sisters gave birth, first to boys: Arthur and, six weeks later, myself. Two years thereafter they both had daughters, one day apart. We were almost like siblings—we might as well have been, since all our blood relatives are common.

Arthur was a harum-scarum little boy, always in trouble, often getting lost in crowds (notably at the 1939 New York World's Fair). "My clothes were always messy and dirty," Arthur has written in a privately printed memoir. "Jay's were always neat and clean." The comparison is apt. A picture of the two of us shows us, at age four, in a pony cart. The animal has just started to pass water. Arthur's mouth is wide open in delight. I am frowning in embarrassed disapproval. My sense of decorum developed early.

During one of our visits to Akn's house, Arthur threw a doughnut into the goldfish bowl: "To save the fish," he explained—the doughnut being, he fancied, a miniature life ring. Akn was not amused.

"That child requires a severe laying on of hands," he announced, using one of his favorite phrases.

On the landing of the main stairway at Akn's house was a bronze statue of the Greek god Mercury, clad only in a detachable fig leaf. As children we delighted to remove the fig leaf, placing it always at the base of the statue. My sense of decorum had limits, even then.

This is clearly the appropriate point for a story of my

grandfather that I heard from my father many years later. One evening in the Newport Reading Room, a men's club, some members who had consumed too many adult beverages were discussing the question proposed by one of their number: why circumcision, practiced for generations, did not become hereditary. Unable to settle the matter, they appealed to the Rector of Trinity Church. My grandfather told them that, on this point, he held, with Shakespeare, that

> There's a divinity who shapes our ends
> Rough-hew them how we will.[7]

I learned early that my father had no great opinion of his father. "Wise in his public life, but invariably foolish in his private affairs," was his characteristic dismissal. A conversational exchange between the two of them remains indelibly in my memory. Akn had just announced that he had been appointed to the Marriage Commission of the Episcopal Diocese of Rhode Island.

"What?" my father exclaimed in a tone of outraged disbelief. "With *your* views on marriage?"

I was shocked. I would never have dared speak to my own father like that.

Akn had a black cook, Melinda, whom we children loved—for the infectious warmth of her laughter and the delicious smells that came from her kitchen. Sunday dinner at Akn's house always concluded with ice cream and a multilayered lemon cake with paper-thin slices of lemon in the icing on top. Children take everything for granted. I thought everyone ate such food. It would be many years before I realized how privileged my childhood was. I salivate even now, remembering that lemon cake. Never have I tasted anything more delectable.

A more serious memory of my grandfather concerns his preaching. Though I often sat beneath his graceful, triple-decked hourglass pulpit in Newport's Trinity Church, I cannot remember any of his sermons. In later years, however, my father told me that his father had been a good preacher. This gives added significance to something my grandfather told me: that he always wrote out his sermons in full. "It is always best," he said.

I agree. Writing forces the preacher to say exactly what he wants to say, and saves him from rambling. A written text also frees the preacher from dependence on a limited stock of familiar phrases and allows him to be more creative. To this day I never preach (save for the brief meditative homilies at daily Mass) without a full written text before me.

But it is time to tell of my maternal grandparents.

* * *

To us children they were Grandpa and Granny: John Clarkson Jay ("Jack") and Marguerite Montgomery Soleliac ("Daisy"). Grandpa had an imposing waistline, the prominent "Jay nose" (visible in pictures of the Chief Justice—and in the mirror to myself), and a bald head. He loved music and played the piano by ear—in a grand thumping style, stamping his left foot in time with the music.

Grandpa and Granny lived in Manhattan in a narrow five-story town house at 120 East Seventy-third Street, between Park and Lexington Avenues. A two-passenger elevator ran from the ground floor to the top, a source of endless delight to children.

Grandpa was a *bon vivant*. A refrigerator in a pantry off the third-floor library was always stocked with champagne, soda water, and ginger ale for the grandchildren. At certain seasons we would also find in it pheasants and wild ducks shot by my grandparents or their friends, still clad in their gorgeous plumage.

After the birds had been eaten, the wishbones were hung to dry on the arms of the lighting fixtures in the second-floor formal dining room. There were scores of them, neatly arranged according to species: tiny squab wishbones, then those taken from ducks, chickens, pheasants, geese, and finally the large turkey wishbones. No meal in that room was complete without the pulling of one of these wishbones with each grandchild.

"Make a wish, Jay," Grandpa or Granny would say. "Now pull."

If you were lucky enough to get the larger piece after the bone snapped, you were supposed to get your wish. I always wished for a pony. I never got one. This I have long ceased to regret. A pony would not have brought me the happiness I imagined in those far-off days.

I recall a birthday party in that house. My grandparents asked me beforehand what kind of entertainment I would like at the party.

"Either a treasure hunt or a magician," I replied.

I could hardly believe my good fortune when, on the great day, I got both. The treasure hunt came first. Each child was given the end of a string and a stick on which to wind it up. The string led all over the house to a present at the end. Afterward a magician entertained us in the drawing room.

The party was an example of one of Grandpa's most endearing characteristics: extravagance. Whenever we visited him he would give us children dimes and quarters. "I find it helps keep the affection of my grandchildren," he explained to my father. Grandpa once mailed me a wrist watch for my birthday, wrapped in an unused roll of sterile absorbent cotton, purchased from a pharmacy for this sole purpose. In later years a family friend told me that when he visited my grandfather to tell of his forthcoming marriage, Grandpa immediately called for champagne—and set aside the first two bottles he opened because they were not to his taste.

At picnics he would pour kerosene on a "ten cent store" hand towel (bought by the dozen at Woolworth's) to light the fire for cooking the hot dogs. These towels had many other uses as well. When his Scotch terrier Nippy got carsick (a frequent occurrence), Grandpa, who kept an ample supply of ten cent store towels with him at all times, used as many as necessary to clean up the mess. A notable polluter (in a pre-ecological age), he threw the soiled towels out the car window.

Grandpa's underpants were linen, bought in Paris and embroidered with his initials by French nuns. In the heady days of the 1920s he voyaged annually to France to replenish the stock while revisiting the land of his Huguenot forebears. Disposal of the worn garments was unproblematic. Grandpa tied them in ten cent store towels and put them through the porthole of his stateroom in mid-Atlantic. It was truly an age of innocence.

Grandpa and Granny would speak French to each other when they wanted to communicate something they did not wish their grandchildren to hear. I still recall the frisson of pleasure I experienced at understanding the words "les enfants" and "aller au Trans-Lux"—a chain of movie theaters in Manhattan that showed a continuous hour-long program of newsreels, cartoons, and short features—a great favorite with children. Though I was not yet nine (my age at my grandmother's death),

I managed to feign pleased surprise when informed, shortly thereafter, that we were indeed to be taken to the Trans-Lux.

Meals at Grandpa's were exceptional—though I would not realize this till I reached my majority. A clearly remembered dessert (which I have never had since) consisted of ice cream in a kind of bird's nest of something called "spun sugar." Some years ago I found the recipe for this delicacy in the *Boston Cookbook*. When I saw that it involved the use of a whisk and a thermometer, I realized that it was beyond my culinary powers.

The butter at Grandpa's was always unsalted. Cream was so thick that it had lumps in it. (No one knew about cholesterol in those days.) How we loved to pour it on our oatmeal at breakfast, sweetening the porridge with brown sugar, so much more interesting for children than ordinary white.

This was at Williamstown, Massachusetts, where Grandpa, a fervent Williams College alumnus, had a modest bungalow on the farm of a friend who raised prize Guernsey cows that produced the cream. Even as children we were impressed with the five-figure prices for which, we were told, these animals were sold. (Today one would surely have to add another zero at least to those figures.)

The Williamstown "Playhouse," as it was called, was the center, for us children, of a realm every bit as enchanted as Akn's house at Newport. How we loved to visit the barns to see the prize cattle in their individual box stalls with the record of milk production hanging over each. The enormous bulls, each with a ring in its nose, were formidable indeed, frightening even behind the solid bars of their pens.

On the lawn in front of the Playhouse, Grandpa and Granny would sometimes shoot clay pigeons, round disks flung heavenward from a spring-driven catapult. One day I was told that I was to accompany them on a real shoot. The quarry was not wild fowl, but frogs. This astonished me. I had never heard of shooting frogs. Nor could I see any reason to do so. Frog legs, I was informed, were good to eat. We returned to the Playhouse with a full bag. Sautéed in garlic butter, they were delicious. I sometimes order them in a restaurant today—unless the menu lists sweetbreads, a delicacy of a higher order altogether for which, with kidneys, I first developed a taste at my maternal grandparents' table.

I am unclear about the financial basis for this lifestyle. Grandpa, I was told, had lost his money in the stock market crash of 1929. A partner in the Wall Street firm of J. and W. Seligman, he had refused to follow the practice of the other partners, who placed their assets in their wives' names. Grandpa considered this dishonorable. When the crash came, it fell more heavily on him than on his colleagues.

He was a director of the Pierce Arrow Motor Company and possessed an automobile of that make, a magnificent two-door convertible with a dashing yellow stripe and his initials on the door. In 1939 he was made President of the Fifth Avenue Bank—an institution long since swallowed up by larger competitors. The bank cultivated a personal relationship with its depositors and ensured that they would be worth cultivating by requiring, at the depth of the Depression, a minimum balance of a thousand dollars (the equivalent today of at least twenty thousand, perhaps far more).

Grandpa loved this job. The feeling in the family was that he had finally come into his own. To everyone's sorrow, his enjoyment of his new position was brief. He died of a coronary thrombosis on January 22, 1941, after less than two years as bank president and only two days after his sixty-first birthday. I was in my first year at boarding school and unable to attend his funeral, a source of keen regret to me then and since.

I clearly recall my grandmother's funeral four years earlier, in June 1937. Grandpa, in striped trousers, cutaway, and a high silk hat encircled with a broad mourning band of black crepe, led us on foot from his 73RD Street house to the Episcopal Church of the Resurrection one block north. At the church door he turned to my cousin Arthur and me and asked, "Which one of you boys is older?"

Upon learning that it was Arthur, Grandpa took him by his right hand, and me by his left—a fine example of the keen sense of propriety I have inherited from him and cherish today. Three abreast, we walked up the aisle behind my grandmother's coffin, borne aloft on the shoulders of six pallbearers—so much more fitting than the tacky undertakers' trolleys used at funerals today.

Four months before that grandfather's own death, on the evening before my initial departure for boarding school, my father took me to a Broadway theater to see the hit play *The Man who Came to Dinner,* with Monty Wooley in the leading role. (I would play the part myself at school a year later, but that is another story.) Whom should we encounter in the lobby during the intermission but Grandpa.

"Dudley," he immediately told his son-in-law, "I knew two minutes after the curtain went up that you were in the theater." We both knew why. Daddy's laugh was loud, uproarious, and unmistakable.

I have always regretted this grandfather's untimely death.

He was as fond of me, I know, as I was of him. A widower since his wife's death in 1937, he was lonely. Had he lived, he would have taken me, as I passed through my teens, to restaurants and the theater and on trips. How we both would have enjoyed that. I have only the happiest memories of Grandpa, a man of boundless humor and fun, and the soul of generosity. My childhood recollections are enhanced by the stories of him I heard from my father. One of them was about Grandpa's business principles.

"When you have good news to give someone," he told my father, "you can write a note, make a phone call, or send a message. Anything difficult or unpleasant requires a personal conversation."

I have tried to follow this principle in my own life. Others, I have found, do not. When I was teaching at a Catholic boarding school in Germany in the early 1960s, it became necessary to send home a teenage boy in my house. I assumed that the headmaster, a priest of the highest integrity, would tell the boy himself. Instead he instructed me, "You tell him, Herr Hughes." I did so. But my respect for my superior was diminished.

* * *

Though I lived, until age twelve, for nine months of the year in Manhattan, it was urban living with a difference. The family apartment consisted of four rooms on the second floor of the Choir School. An early memory, probably from age four or five, is of my parents about to depart for a dinner party: my mother in an elegant, long evening gown, my father in a tail coat, clerical collar above a black silk waistcoat, and a top hat.

How handsome they looked! And how far off that vanished world seems today.

A less pleasant memory was the kidnapping of the Lindbergh baby in March 1932, two months before my fourth birthday. Impressed by the hushed tones in which I heard the grownups discussing this crime, I asked my mother if the kidnapper was not "very naughty."

"He wasn't naughty, Jay," she told me, "he was wicked"—intending, I understood at the time, by the use of this (to me) unfamiliar word to indicate a depth of iniquity to which her eldest son had not yet sunk.

For a time I feared being kidnapped myself. Above my bed in the nursery was a terra cotta reproduction of the infant Jesus by Della Robbia. Since this hung by a single strand of wire from the molding near the ceiling, the breeze from the open window nearby made it rattle against the wall. Hearing this noise as I lay in bed awaiting sleep, I imagined it was a kidnapper climbing through the window to carry me off. The reflection that I was an unlikely target for kidnapping since "Daddy and Mummy don't have much money," failed to banish the fears that troubled me nightly—and which it never occurred to me to mention to my parents. Who ever said that childhood was carefree?

The choir boys made pets of us three children, playing with us and our cocker spaniel dog whenever they were free. From an early age I knew all the boys by name. Entering the school myself at age nine was the most natural thing in the world. Having outgrown the nursery, I simply moved down the hall into an alcove in one of the two dormitories. But this is jumping ahead.

What made our experience of city living unique was that

when we went outdoors we were not in city streets, but in the Cathedral Close. This was a large park containing, in addition to the cathedral (already in its uncompleted state the largest church building in North America at more than a tenth of a mile in length), the Synod House, an open-air pulpit, the Deanery, and Bishop's House. This magnificent structure had been built in the style of a French chateau by a cathedral trustee, the elder J.P. Morgan. When critics objected that the bishop did not need fifty-seven rooms, Morgan would hear none of it. "The bishop," he said, "should live like everyone else in New York."

The occupant of that office from 1921 until his retirement in 1946 at the age of eighty-one was William Thomas Manning. Small in stature but great in the power of his convictions and the firmness with which he expressed them, Bishop Manning was a major civic figure in New York (mentioned in the Cole Porter song *You're the Top* and regularly in the *New York Times*), as well as the chief shepherd of the flock on whose behalf he expended the last reserves of his considerable powers. He was an intimate friend of our family and the greatest hero of my youth. The Episcopal Church has not seen his equal since his death in 1949.

The Bishop's House, to which we children had free access, was a magical kingdom to us. In it resided, in addition to the bishop, his wife, and their maiden daughter, Frances—my godmother and, to us children, always "Aunt Frances." Sunday dinner at the Bishop's House was a regular feature of my childhood. Shortly before one o'clock the three of us children would walk the fifty yards from the Choir School to the Bishop's House, carrying in a special pouch a bib and a set of child's cutlery for Dudley. This included a silver "pusher": a small utensil shaped like a hoe, with which the child was supposed to maneuver his food onto fork or spoon.

"Do we have Dudley's pusher?" Jane and I regularly asked each other, as we started on these weekly expeditions. The question was an unending source of mirth, rooted no doubt in our sense of superiority at having left such relics of infancy behind us.

Having rung the bell at the Bishop's House, we would be admitted by a uniformed maid, sometimes by Aunt Frances. Then came the long climb up the broad marble staircase with a thick velvet rope hanging from rings on the left-hand side in place of a railing. At the top was the immense dining room. First, however, we walked down the broad second-floor hallway to the formal drawing room at the farther end. There we were greeted by Mrs. Manning and the Bishop. The stone in his episcopal ring rattled as he patted our heads.

"Oh, William, you're hurting the children," Mrs. Manning would say. The ring did hurt a little. But I liked that pat on the head nonetheless. On the way into dinner we would sometimes detour through two smaller (but still large) reception rooms off the hall. In one was a grand piano surmounted by signed portraits of European royalty.

Surroundings such as these, combined with the towering personality of Bishop Manning and the deeply impressive services on great occasions in the magnificent cathedral next door, gave me an exaggerated notion of the centrality of Anglicanism in world Christendom, which would not be dispelled for decades.

Next door to the Bishop's House was the Deanery, the residence until his death in 1939 of the Very Reverend Milo Hudson Gates and his invalid wife, "Pussy." There too we children were warmly welcomed, though our visits were infrequent. My father's opinion of this dignitary was quite different from his regard for Bishop Manning.

"Jay, I have something I need to speak to you about," my father said to me one day. Never in my experience had anything good ever followed from this opening. Nor did it on this occasion.

"I understand that you told Grandpa that 'Dean Gates is a fool.'"

I could not deny it.

"Yes," my father continued, "well you may have heard me say that. But you must never say that kind of thing to other people."

It was my first experience of "Do as I say and not as I do."

That I should have repeated my father's dismissal of his colleague is hardly surprising. He was not a man to suffer fools gladly. The number of those who fell within that category was legion.

"He's no ordinary fool!" my father would thunder.

Decades later this judgment about a superior, repeated too often and too openly, would cost my father the deanship of another cathedral. (That the epithet, in this case, was richly deserved was, understandably, no defense.)

A childhood incident of which I have no recollection, but which is frequently repeated in the family, has me telling my maternal grandfather at an early age:

"All Daddy's friends are fools."

3

"Mummy is Dead."

At age five I was enrolled in New York's Trinity School, going straight into the first grade without having attended kindergarten. Decades later my first day at school would figure in one of my published homilies, on the text: "See, I make all things new" (Revelation 21:5).

> Few things are more devastating for a small child than to be suddenly separated from Mummy or Daddy. Across the span of half a century, I can still recall my feeling of panic when, on my first day at school, I found that my mother had slipped away without my noticing. I realize now that she wanted to spare me a tearful farewell. At the time, however, I was devastated.

All of us have had similar childhood experiences, I reminded my hearers. We carry them into adult life, fearing that we shall be hurt again; that our efforts at friendship and love will be rebuffed, that we shall be let down, hurt, or abandoned by someone we love and trust. When we are, the old wound is reopened, and our fear of loneliness is reinforced.

I used this common experience as a basis for the preacher's fundamental task: to proclaim good news.

> To those oppressed by loneliness (and which of us is not, at some time or another?) the Lord proclaims: "See, I make all things new."
>
> When no one else understands, there is One who does understand.
>
> When everyone else seems to ignore us, there is One who accepts us.
>
> When I cannot find one other person to accept the love I long to give, there is One who does accept: who loved me *before* I loved him, who loves me more than I can ever love him, who will go on loving me no matter what.
>
> His name is Jesus Christ. He is the One who makes all things new.[8]

* * *

I completed my sixth year and the first grade in May 1934. That summer my parents rented a large three-story house on Newport's Washington Street. The back porch looked out on the inner harbor. At a mooring near the private pier that went with the house was our Newport Yacht Club dory *Typhoon.* Sailing one day with my parents in this small open craft, we heeled over so far in a squall that green water poured in over the lee rail. I screamed in terror, certain that our last hour had struck.

"Jay, be quiet," my father shouted at me indignantly. We did not capsize. We didn't even fill. My fear was unfounded and my father's rebuke justified. But I had made an important discovery. I was something my father often mentioned in tones of scornful contempt: a fair-weather sailor. Though I have since learned to love sailing, spending whole weeks and even months on the ocean wave, sailing some ten thousand miles in northern Europe in two boats of my own and once crossing the Atlantic under sail, I have never been able to pretend that I was enjoying myself when wet or terrified. At sea in my father's company I was frequently both. I developed an early antipathy to his cheerfulness in the midst of discomfort and wondered how he could be so different.

I have since been heartened to learn that there are seamen more accomplished than either of us who are also fair-weather sailors. "I prefer it calm," the late world-renowned Captain Irving Johnson told me in the great cabin of his beautiful ketch *Yankee* in a Swedish harbor some four decades ago. And referring to his youthful passages under sail around Cape Horn, he added, "You couldn't buy me to go there today." Now there's a man after my own heart.

Another clearly remembered moment of terror from that summer happened on land. My mother had brought home a bag of live lobsters, which broke, spilling its contents on the kitchen floor, where the crustaceans crawled rapidly in all directions. I ran screaming from the room, certain that my mother was going to be eaten alive. She fetched me back with a laugh, assuring me that the claws were tied and that neither of us was in any danger.

Back in New York that autumn I was now a sophisticated second-grader. In December I had a speaking part in the school's pre-Christmas program. I was proud to see my mother in the audience. The auditorium was overheated and she caught a cold. My next recollection is of the doctor's visit and my mother sitting in an armchair in the living room of our Choir School apartment with a thermometer in her mouth. I was told that she would have to go to the hospital. An ambulance was summoned. The attendants carried Mummy out of the apartment on a stretcher. I cried. When you are only six and they carry your mother away on a stretcher, you cry.

Later that day Daddy came back from St. Luke's Hospital, across the street from the Cathedral, and told us three children that Mummy had pneumonia. It was a serious disease, he explained, and people sometimes died of it. (It was before antibiotics. Sulfa drugs had been discovered, but would not be used clinically in the United States until 1936.) We would pray, however, that God would make her well. I recall going over to the Cathedral with our Irish nurse, Kitty, and praying in the "Children's Corner" (the somewhat half-hearted attempt at folk religion found in many Anglican cathedrals) for Mummy to get well.

She got worse. A few days before Christmas, Daddy gave us children the presents our mother had got for us and told us we could open them early. My gifts were a leather jacket and a Book of Common Prayer (containing the Anglican liturgy) bound in red leather, with my name in gold on the cover. (I have it still, rebound.) Then he took us to the hospital to see Mummy.

He explained that she was in an oxygen tent, which helped her to breathe. We were not permitted to enter her room, but looked in at her through the glass window in the door. I pointed to the leather jacket she had given me, which I was wearing, held up the prayer book with one hand, and waved with the other. She waved back and smiled. How beautiful she looked.

Christmas dinner at Grandpa's house on 73RD Street was shadowed by anxiety over Mummy's grave illness. I remember the grownups saying that we could not have thirteen at table (the number at Jesus' Last Supper). If my mother's younger brother John got home in time to join us, a kitchen maid would join us to make us fourteen.

The day after Christmas, about five o'clock in the afternoon, Daddy came into our apartment at the Choir School with Bishop Manning and another priest-friend, Dr. Spear. He called the three of us children together and, seated in the same armchair where Mummy had sat a week before to have her temperature taken, he told us: "Children, Mummy is dead. Jay, you will understand. And I think you can too, Jane. Dudley, you're too young. We'll never hear Mummy's voice again. She'll never be with us again in these rooms. She'll never use her things. Here I am crying with you." It was the only time I ever saw my father cry.

My whole world had collapsed. From this blow I have never fully recovered. I belong today to the walking wounded.

In the days following, my mother's body lay in St. James' Chapel in the Cathedral in the plain wooden coffin made for her by the cathedral carpenters. Each day my father celebrated Mass there for the repose of her soul. I attended.

The funeral was celebrated before the high altar of the cathedral, with the full choir of men and boys providing the music and Bishop Manning officiating along with my father and Dr. Spear. At the end, six men carried the coffin on their shoulders the whole length of the cathedral nave, down the steps at the west door, and placed it in the waiting hearse.

The scene in the Jay family cemetery at Rye, New York, remains indelibly fixed in my memory. The coffin was lowered on straps to the bottom of the grave and Bishop Manning had the committal. To the accompaniment of the solemn words from the Book of Common Prayer, "Earth to earth, ashes to ashes, dust to dust," my father cast shovelfuls of earth into grave. The dull thump of the heavy clods raining down on the coffin lid was the most terrible sound I have ever heard.

Within days of the funeral my father said we must still pray for Mummy. She was with God. He was taking care of her. Our prayers, the best expression of our love for her, could still help her. That made sense to me at age six. It makes sense to me today.

We would often visit the cemetery in the years following. The three of us children would stand by our mother's grave (not thirty feet from that of the Chief Justice) while Daddy said a prayer for the repose of her soul. Then he would lead us in the Our Father. I was never able to finish it.

In time a simple upright stone was erected, rounded at the top. Under my mother's name and dates, and the words, "Beloved wife of The Rev'd William Dudley Foulke Hughes," was a Latin inscription, I think from Horace: *I nimium dilecta, I bona parts animae meae. Ego maerens disco sequi.* The same words, untranslated, appear on the tombstone of my father's mother in the churchyard of Trinity Church, Newport. In deference to a wish of my maternal grandfather, my father placed a translation of the words on the back of my mother's stone, in English verse:

Pass hence, beloved, leaving the path we twain have trod.

Pass, and the soul that still is one with thine,

through grief will learn to follow thee to God.

* * *

Never in the more than seventy years since this tragedy have I ever said, or ever permitted anyone else to say, "It was God's will." My mother's death was not God's will. What kind of a God would that be who would rob a devoted young husband and father of his twenty-seven-year-old wife, and three small children of their mother? My mother's death was a mystery—a dark mystery. Yet God, who as Solomon said in his prayer for the dedication of the Jerusalem Temple, "has chosen to dwell in thick darkness" (1 Kings 8:12), was in this mystery.

I can no longer recall the exact day when I discovered God in the darkness. I can fix it, however, before the age of nine. One day I realized that the parting was not forever. With blinding certainty it came home to me that I would see my mother again, when God called me home. From that day to this the unseen spiritual world—the world of God, of the angels, of the saints, and of our beloved dead—has been real to me. I know people who are there: my mother first, and now so many others whom God has called home to himself. Decades later I realized that this insight was the beginning of my priestly vocation. It kindled in me the desire to be close to that spiritual world.

I resonate to the self-chosen epitaph of the nineteenth century English convert Cardinal John Henry Newman: *Ex umbris et imaginibus in veritatem*: "Out of shadows and images into the truth"—into the true world, the eternal world which, unlike this world of time and sense, is not passing away, and never can. At the altar I stand on the threshold of that world. There, there is no darkness. There, as we read twice over in the Bible's final book, "God will wipe away all tears from our eyes" (Revelation 7:17 and 21:4).

4
Choirboy

In later years my father told me that I had had an unusually close relationship with my mother. Following her death I transferred to him all the affection I had had for her. This was perhaps inevitable. But it would cause difficulties later on, delaying my achievement of the emotional independence necessary for maturity.

At age nine, I entered the Cathedral Choir School. This involved participation in the cathedral liturgies: Matins or Morning Prayer in St. Ambrose Chapel, and sung Evensong in the Great Choir. I thus acquired familiarity with the Psalms and considerable stretches of the Old and New Testaments, which has enriched my life ever since.

Since earliest childhood, public worship has been as natural to me as eating and sleeping. I often accompanied my father when he celebrated an early weekday Mass in one of the cathedral chapels. He would try to teach me the names of the vestments as he put them on in the sacristy: amice, alb, cincture, stole, maniple, and chasuble. To his dismay, the only one my child's brain could retain was "stole." So this must have been before I started school at age five.

In the penitential seasons of Advent and Lent, Episcopalians of that era were accustomed to recite, before the final blessing at Mass, the Eucharistic hymn *O Saving Victim*. The second stanza contains the line: "Forevermore, blest One in three." Before learning to read, I understood this not as a reference to the Trinity but as a prayer: "Bless one in three." This seemed to me entirely reasonable. Given the undeniable fact of human sin, God (I reasoned) could hardly be expected to bless everyone. But he could at least be asked to bless one out of three.

When, as a choirboy, I started to attend daily Matins, some of the readings made a strong impression on me. I was particularly struck by the repeated cycle of the Israelites' rebellion against God during their desert wanderings, following their deliverance from Egypt. I noted that this was followed, each time, by divine retribution, repentance, and forgiveness. The people's behavior struck me as remarkably obtuse. They seemed never to learn. One day I realized that this pattern was repeated in every life, my own included. Years later I would learn that this was the consequence of original sin: that flaw in our nature that causes us, knowing the difference between good and evil, and that we should choose good and reject evil, often to do the opposite. Original sin is the easiest of all Christian doctrines to prove, since it can be verified in daily experience.

During Lent my father, as headmaster, read to us during Matins selections from Bunyan's *Pilgrim's Progress*. I found them riveting. When at the end, Mr. Valiant-for-Truth went into the river saying, "Death, where is thy sting?" and "Grave, where is thy victory?" and then "All the trumpets sounded for him on the other side," I had goose bumps.

I started to serve at the altar before I entered the Choir School. Since I was too small for any of the vestments in the sacristy cupboard, I wore street clothes. This offended my sense of propriety. I was thankful when growth terminated my embarrassment.

A small Prayer Book still in my possession, signed by Bishop Manning, attests that he confirmed me in the cathedral in Holy Week, on March 22, 1937, shortly before my ninth birthday. My First Communion was postponed until Pentecost; why, I do not know. My father had obtained the bishop's permission for me to receive these sacraments several years before the customary age.

The liturgy and canon law of the Catholic Church still envisage this ancient sequence for the sacraments of initiation: Baptism, Confirmation, Eucharist. This order is almost universally reversed in practice, however, by admitting very young children to Communion and postponing Confirmation until later—often years later. I am reminded of this anomaly each time I baptize a child and find myself saying of the new Christian: "In Confirmation he/she will receive the fullness of God's Spirit. In Holy Communion he/she will share the banquet of Christ's sacrifice ... " It grates on my sensibility to utter what I know to be palpable nonsense. My clerical colleagues appear to be untroubled.

As choirboys we wore high starched Eton collars three inches wide, neckties, and suits—short pants for boys in the lower school, long for their seniors. We marched in step double file to the daily cathedral services under the leadership of older boy prefects who called out the time, "Hip, hip." On top of the uniform described above we wore, on these occasions, short black academic gowns and mortarboards.

At daily choir practices we learned to sing Gregorian plainchant, Anglican chant (harmonized), Palestrina (which I hated), and anthems and operatic Masses (which I loved). I remember especially Mozart's *Ave Verum,* choruses from Handel's *Messiah* and the Brahms *Requiem*, and Gounod's *St. Cecilia Mass,* which carried us two octaves above middle C. When I was allowed to sing the soprano solo in Mendelssohn's richly romantic *Oh, for the Wings of a Dove,* I thought I had gone to heaven without dying.

I had piano lessons from an early age. As a choirboy I started organ lessons with our English-born Choirmaster, Norman Coke-Jephcott. After two years I could play the simpler preludes and fugues from the Bach *Little Organ Book* and his lyrical *Jesu, Joy of Man's Desiring.* Twice I was permitted to play the organ postlude on the great cathedral organ after weekday Evensong—an exciting but unnerving experience, since the interval between pressing the keys and hearing the sound in the vast space required close attention to the tempo while ignoring the sound. The organs I had played on previously were in the cathedral chapels, where there was no such interval.

I would continue to play the organ at boarding school and college. Today I can barely stumble through a hymn. For this modest ability there is now, alas, little demand, given the banal Hallmark "songs" that pass for sacred music in all too many Catholic parishes in the United States. Talking recently with a classically trained Catholic organist who battles valiantly to stop the rot, I told him of my early training and bemoaned the loss of the grand and stirring hymnody that formed my musical taste. "Ah, but you were spoiled," he responded.

Of the academic training at the Choir School, I remember that it included Latin from the start, taught, among others, by my father. In recent years alumni who were at the school with me have told me it was the best school they ever attended. I cherish particularly the tribute to my father of one contemporary.

> I had a gorgeous time at the Choir School. The education offered was straightforward stuff which has remained with me for fifty years. Dudley Hughes was one of the last of the old schoolmasters. He could fill in for any of his teachers turned sick—to do French or math or Latin—with perfect aplomb, and his introduction to English and Church history I still use. But what I liked best was his attitude toward discipline: good-humored, hard-hitting, and no sentimental fussing around. If he caught us up on the cathedral roof, it was short rations and study hall all through the weekend, but no recriminations. He didn't really think it was bad, just dangerous.

* * *

At age eleven I passed into the upper school and graduated to long trousers. Once a week we older boys went to dancing class. For this we wore navy blue suits and white gloves. My emotions, always vulnerable, were soon conquered by a dark-haired beauty who reciprocated my affection by returning the squeezes I gave her through our two pairs of gloves.

In some way, which I can no longer recall, I arranged for

her to visit me in our apartment at the Choir School. As we sat together on the living room sofa I managed, greatly daring, to kiss her on the cheek. I was mortified to discover shortly thereafter that our nurse, Kitty, had observed us through a crack in the door, left carefully ajar for this purpose.

This early infatuation had an unhappy denouement later on when I went away to boarding school. The girl's mother wrote me repeatedly, entreating me to write her daughter, who was suffering the pangs of unrequited love. I complied as best I could. But it was not easy. That fire had gone out.

No less an authority than the Apostle Paul has told us that "It is better to marry than to burn" (1 Corinthians 7:9). I have no experience of matrimony. But I have been familiar with its alternative from earliest childhood. Even before my mother's death (when I was six), certain boys in the Choir School, with whom I fraternized daily years before I joined their ranks, kindled in me feelings of excitement, and physical stirrings as well, which I realized years later were sexual.

As a choirboy myself, I had intense emotional friendships with several of my peers and a long-lasting relationship with one, a year or two older, which was terminated only when he transferred his affections to a male university student who supervised our afternoon team sports. I suffered agonies of heartbreak and jealousy in consequence.

Had this happened decades later, the friend who abandoned me for an older and more interesting admirer might well have been persuaded years later to join the burgeoning army of "victims" demanding compensation for their youthful emotional distress. In that case, the Choir School, and my father as headmaster, could have faced a lawsuit alleging gross negligence in employing a sexually abusive athletic coach. Instead, my friend has been "happily married for thirty-nine years" (as he wrote me in a 1989 letter, our first contact in half a century) with three grown children and six grandchildren. Without wishing for a moment to minimize the grave evil of sexual abuse of the young, I ask the reader to reflect whether the way my friend dealt his own youthful emotional turmoil might not be more fruitful than the currently popular exploitation of victimhood.

Attraction to my own sex was never exclusive. Then and since I was also drawn strongly to girls. I do not know the etiology of homosexuality. Nor do those who claim to be experts. Some contend that it is genetic, others that it is the result of experiences in early childhood. To one thing, however, I can testify from personal experience. The orientation itself is given, not chosen. Who would chose something that brings only misunderstanding at best and—at worst and far more often—opprobrium, hatred, and persecution?

Persecution of men with this orientation is due to what is today called homophobia: the fear in some men of their feminine side. This fear is itself "objectively disordered" (to use a term applied by the *Catechism of the Catholic Church* to the homosexual orientation). We are all in some degree mixtures of feminine and masculine. Even the most masculine man has one or two feminine qualities, and the most feminine woman masculine ones.

I am who I am, and thankful for it: the man a gracious and loving Creator has made me—through my parents and my experience of life. The *Catechism* gets it right when it says that "the number of men and women who have deep-seated homosexual tendencies is not negligible," and that it "constitutes for most of them a trial. They must be accepted with respect, compassion, and sensitivity. Every sign of unjust discrimination in their regard should be avoided" (No. 2358).

* * *

Boys had to leave the Choir School when their voices changed. This happened to me at age eleven. In September 1940, four months after my twelfth birthday, I entered South Kent School in northwestern Connecticut. One of the things I took with me was a safety razor. I would soon be using it daily. It was the end of my childhood.

5

Boarding School

South Kent School had been founded in 1923 by Sam Bartlett and Dick Cuyler, two alumni of the better known and larger Kent School, a few miles to the north. It was a no-frills, spartan institution. An oft told tale of the school's early days recounted how a boy, wishing to demonstrate the quality of the school food, slapped an address label on a breakfast pancake and mailed it home. It arrived intact.

The school's distinguishing feature was the "self-help" system. Boys did all the cleaning and maintenance work inside and out, save that which required adult expertise. In my day the only paid help for a community of 120 consisted of two cooks and the man who looked after the electrical and plumbing systems. Our headmaster, Sam Bartlett, explained that the object was not to save money. We did the work ourselves because it was philosophically right.

"Gentlemen," he would say (using the form of address from which he never varied), "what have you accomplished at age fifteen or sixteen or seventeen that entitles you to expect adults to wait on you?"

The answer was obvious, even to adolescents. Bartlett's lesson affected me deeply. The view of the world, and of my place in it, which I learned from him was counter-cultural even then. Today it would rank right up there with the Flat Earth theory. How many of today's parents would be willing to risk the disapproval of their peers, and the alienation of their offspring, by questioning the assumption that adults exist to maintain a taxi service for the young and to finance their vacations and hobbies?

Sam Bartlett was an example of New England Puritanism at its best, supported by the Anglo-Catholic faith he had learned as a schoolboy from his own headmaster, Father Sill, founder of Kent School and a monk of the Episcopal Order of the Holy Cross. Bartlett was a daily communicant. When I was assigned cleaning duties in the chapel, I regularly saw him sitting for twenty minutes and more in the back pew before the evening chapel service, his unblinking gaze on the crucifix above the altar tabernacle. This helped me understand the story I read years later about the nineteenth-century French priest St. Jean Vianney asking a peasant farmer what he did during his daily visits to the parish church in Ars without prayer book or rosary, his lips unmoving.

"I look at him," the man responded, "and he looks at me."

When I read that, I remembered my old headmaster. I count it among the chief blessings of a richly blessed life to have achieved, past middle life, some approximation of this prayer myself.

Bartlett's son, George, for a time a South Kent headmaster himself, recalls that during the Second World War his father would spend up to a half hour daily praying for "his boys" in danger overseas:

"Until Father Sill died, Sam visited him regularly to make his confession. He was always happier coming home. We five children kidded him about many things, but never about his faith. That was his rock."

* * *

I made my own first confession in the South Kent chapel, toward the end of my first year at the school. Sacramental confession is voluntary for Anglicans. Many are unaware of the sacrament's existence. It soon became a crucial element in my spiritual development. Despite constant falls, I never failed to find comfort and strength in the priest's words: "And by the authority committed to me I absolve you from your sins in the name of the Father, and of the Son, and of the Holy Spirit. Go in peace, the Lord has put away all your sins."

Two decades later I was appalled to discover that Catholics heard nothing—because they were busy obeying the priest's direction to "make a good, sincere act of contrition," while he whispered something in Latin. The words of absolution should be heard. Now that they are in the vernacular, they can be understood.

I cannot imagine my life without the sacrament of penance. This, more than anything else, gave me courage to become a priest. Without it I could never have remained a priest. Sacramental confession is not, as many Catholics suppose, merely an unpleasant duty, like going to the dentist: something we dislike, but know is good for us, and which makes us feel better afterward. It is a personal encounter with someone who loves us more than we can ever imagine, who is always near us, no matter how far we stray from him. His name is Jesus Christ.

Around the time of my first confession, I joined what Catholics would call a sodality: the Servants of Christ the King. Members undertook to follow a rule of life: daily morning and evening prayer; grace before meals; weekly Mass and Communion; monthly confession; observance of the Friday abstinence from meat; and on five days each week, ten minutes of mental prayer (discursive meditation, for which a handbook containing the rule and prayers gave simple directions). Members graded their own observance of this rule on a scale of one to ten in an annual written report to the director, a Holy Cross monk, and received a friendly note of admonition and encouragement in response.

It was faithfulness to this rule of mental prayer which gave me, at age fifteen, the closest approximation to a religious experience I have ever had. During the summer before my final year at school, I had my first paid job, working in the photostat department of a Wall Street bank. (The Xerox machine had not yet been invented.) During my lunch hour, I would visit Trinity Episcopal Church on Broadway at the head of Wall Street. In the Blessed Sacrament chapel to the right of the high altar, I made my daily meditation.

Kneeling there one day, I became aware of the chorus of prayer and praise ascending at that moment from convent and monastery chapels all over the world to the God whom I, too, was struggling to worship. My prayer, so full of distractions and mostly so dry, was a tiny drop in a vast ocean.

That was all. There were no voices, no intense feelings, certainly nothing like a vision. But at the time it was very real to me and brought me inner joy and peace. Sixty-four years of perseverance in prayer since then have brought me nothing more. For that I have no regrets. A wise and generous God has given me something better: unshakable, rocklike faith. For those so blessed, religious experiences are superfluous.

From age twelve I knew that I wanted to be a priest. Required during my first year at South Kent to write an essay on "What I expect to be doing in twenty years," I wrote about serving as a missionary in Africa. This idea, to which I had previously devoted not a moment's thought, must have come from the school chaplain, a priest of the Order of the Holy Cross, which had a mission in Liberia.

Once formulated, the idea of priesthood became a settled resident in my mind. As already mentioned, I thought each time I served Mass: *One day I'll stand there.* The thought of a missionary vocation soon disappeared. But priesthood never. I went straight toward that goal, like a steel needle to a magnet, until, twelve years later, I achieved it.

This too I count among my chief blessings. Even then few young people had any clear idea of how they wanted to spend their lives. How much less today, when many remain drifting at the end of their twenties and beyond. Our chaotic age is not conducive to clarity about commitment to lifelong goals.

From the start I spoke openly of my own goal. For as long as memory runs, I have wanted to be different. Announcing my decision for priesthood was a way to satisfy this not entirely admirable desire. Refusing to smoke was another. My peers thought puffing on cigarettes made them look grown up. I thought they looked stupid.

Academic work came easily to me, and I got top marks in

exams with little effort. The only aspect of school life which I disliked was what I considered the overemphasis of athletics. If the school won a football game, euphoria reigned. If we lost, the atmosphere was grim, and the football jocks were in such a foul mood that no one could speak to them. To me athletics were "only a game." The real purpose of school, clearly, was to get an education. That one could also be educated on a playing field never occurred to me. If it had, I would have rejected the idea out of hand.

With this sole exception, I loved my four years at boarding school. Indeed, I can remember a conscious feeling of well-being at South Kent, at times even of euphoria, which would not return until I was past sixty. Never once was I homesick. I did find, however, that absence from home intensifed my already strong love for my family, in particular for my father. I recall as if it were yesterday the thrill of excitement and joy I always felt when, coming off the train which had brought me at the end of term from South Kent to New York, I caught sight of my father in his shovel hat and clerical collar awaiting me on the platform of Grand Central Station.

From time to time he would drive to the school on a week-end with my sister Jane and brother Dudley, bringing a picnic lunch. In early 1941 he wrote that on the following Saturday he would be bringing a widow whom he wanted me to meet, a Mrs. Otis. This announcement did not seem to me significant. At age twelve I was still too young, and far too naïve, to suspect that she would change our lives forever.

6

"I Told You She'd Amuse You."

Of this picnic lunch I have no recollection. A few weeks later I came home (now the rectory of Grace Church, Hastings-on Hudson, whither my father had moved from the New York Cathedral six months earlier) for the spring holidays. My father told me that he had asked Mrs. Otis to marry him, and that she had accepted. I wept—not from unhappiness, but because my father's announcement reopened the still unhealed wound of my mother's death six years earlier. As soon as I was able to speak, I told my father: "I have always prayed that you would marry again."

Had I really done so? I cannot say. I know, however, that I was not dissembling. Telling my father that I had prayed that he would remarry was the only way I knew of assuring him that I truly rejoiced at his news.

"No one can ever replace Mummy," my father said. "She won't be your mother. She'll be your stepmother. She wants you children to call her Bina." This nickname (pronounced to rhyme with "China") had been given her years before by her younger sister, Lois, married to a Jay cousin of mine, John Jay Schieffelin. It was Lois and Jay who had introduced Bina to my father, hoping that they would take to each other.

The matchmaking succeeded. Within weeks of meeting, Daddy and Bina were engaged. My father was not alone in succumbing to her charms. Years later an older St. Louis friend who had just met Bina remarked to me, "Your father never had a prayer."

Bina (born Frances Lindon Smith) had been born in 1903, four years before my mother, as the second of three daughters of the Boston artist and Egyptologist Joseph Lindon Smith and his wife, Corinna Putnam, a daughter of the publishing family. In January 1928 Bina married the Yale graduate Raymond Otis, son of a Chicago banker. The couple settled in Santa Fe, New Mexico, where Ray wrote three novels about the local Indians and Hispanics and joined with Bina in the activities of the local colony of artists and writers. They had no children. Following Ray's death in 1938, at the age of thirty-eight, Bina divided her time between her modest adobe house in Santa Fe and an even more modest apartment under the Third Avenue elevated railroad in New York City.

I spent a night there only days after hearing my father's momentous news, sleeping fitfully on a sofa, while the trains rumbled past outside an open window. The stated purpose of this visit was for Bina and me to get to know each other, and for her to help me shop for additions to my wardrobe at Macy's department store.

I found Bina the most nondirective adult I had ever encountered. We related to each other almost as peers—something I found odd, but also agreeable. Though not yet thirteen, I was already accustomed to traveling alone on the New York subway and to shopping independently at Macy's. While I selected the items I needed, Bina simply observed.

Back at home in Hastings I found my father a changed man. He had always laughed often. Now, however, he seemed ten years younger. I realized how lonely he had been during his six years as a widower. Always a generous contributor to the coffers of "Ma Bell" (before American courts broke up the world's best telephone network), my father spent hours calling relatives and friends throughout the country to tell them of his change of fortune. One statement resounded like a refrain through all these conversations: "I got her through an agency. It's the best way." (When calling long distance, he always raised his voice; his end of the conversation could be heard throughout the house.)

"Rowland, I'm in trouble," he told his charming and generous younger brother in Philadelphia. "Just when I've started on this new job here in Hastings and things seemed to be going well, I find that I'm engaged to be married." Before my uncle realized that his leg was being pulled, he had offered to get on the next train north to offer fraternal support, should rescue prove impossible.

On May 7, 1941, a week before my thirteenth birthday, Daddy and Bina were married by Bishop Manning in the Manhattan Church of St. Edward the Martyr on 109TH Street, just east of Fifth Avenue. I served as acolyte. My brother, Dudley, aged eight and still in short pants, was Best Man.

We soon discovered in Bina an inexhaustible source of laughter and fun. From the start she introduced herself to relatives and friends by saying, "And I'm the wicked stepmother." (Years later she affixed to her refrigerator a magnet with the words: "Wicked stepmother in freezer.") At luncheon only weeks after she had joined the family, my father, telling a story about one of the *grandes dames* of Newport summer society, sent one of his children to fetch the *Social Register*. When he had found the lady in question, he announced:

"She was a Dresser."

"Ooh!" Bina interjected, interrupting the inexorable flow of my father's narrative—something none of his children would ever have dared to do. "Was she a *looker*?"

When the pandemonium unleashed by this remark, so different from the kind of humor to which we children were accustomed, had subsided, my father commented: "I told you she'd amuse you. That's why I got her."

Bina was still amusing us over a half century later. In her late eighties, she took to wearing a button that said, "I'm a legend in my own time." When I telephoned her on her ninety-first birthday, she told me: "In my youth I used to think that something wonderful would happen on my birthday. I thought I would look in the mirror and discover that I was beautiful. I can't remember when I abandoned this fantasy."

7
Harvard

My South Kent diploma contained a personal message handwritten by Headmaster Bartlett:

"May the dear Lord see fit to bless you, Jay; you yourself as a man, and your work as a priest in a life of loving service for Him who has seen fit to call you."

I was just three weeks past my sixteenth birthday when I entered Harvard—too young for college (though I would not realize this until much later). I should have stayed at school another year at least. The American school system makes no provision for this, however. And I was impatient to move on.

For this there were two reasons. First, I was never really a teenager. By age thirteen at the latest I had decided that adults were far more interesting than my peers. My interest in the adult world had started earlier still. By age eight I was reading the headlines in the *New York Times,* and the occasional article. Our nurse, Kitty, once found me crying inconsolably. When she asked me why, I refused to answer, fearing that I would be laughed at. I was distressed because I knew that a terrible war was coming in Europe. The basis for this conviction? What I had read in the paper about Adolf Hitler. This cannot have been later than 1937, the year I turned nine.

After the war started, our family spent several summers with Tom and Julie Matthews, and their four boys, in their Rhode Island summer home "Boothden" (named for its original owner, Edwin Booth, the brother of Lincoln's assassin). Successively book reviewer, managing editor, and editor of *Time* magazine, T.S. Matthews often had journalists and authors as weekend guests, among them the English writer Robert Graves. I listened, enthralled, to their conversation on politics, art, and culture.

When Tom Matthews' father, Episcopal Bishop Paul Matthews of New Jersey, came, my father engaged him on church topics. I found these exchanges, as well as those my father often held with clerical friends in New York, riveting.

The second reason for my impatience to move on to college was the war itself. With the military draft looming at age eighteen, it seemed important to get as much education as possible before the military took me. (In the event, this never happened.) Harvard, to which I had applied at the urging of my father (A Princeton graduate, he often said he hoped one of his sons "would have enough sense to go to Harvard."), admitted me to its freshman class in April 1944. To Harvard I went, therefore, at the beginning of July 1944. (The university had instituted an accelerated wartime schedule, with three semesters annually.)

Harvard initiated me into college life at something called the Freshman Smoker—presumably because of the free cigarettes distributed to those attending, though as a non-smoker I have no recollection of this. I do remember the free flow of beer, however, a talk about what would today be called safe sex, and a story about Abbot Lawrence Lowell, Harvard's president from 1909 to 1933. Today the tale seems tame. In 1944, however, it made a deep impression on us neophytes, convincing us when we heard its then scandalous conclusion that we had arrived in the Big World, where men were men and the world was our oyster.

The story recounted President Lowell's efforts to prevent the building of a subway station in Harvard Square. The contest dragged on for weeks, Lowell contending that the proposed structure would disfigure the square, his opponents countering that the space was undistinguished and other sites impractical. At the height of the battle, we were told, one of the Boston papers appeared with the front page banner headline: *President Lowell Fights Erection in Harvard Square.* The roar of shocked laughter from five hundred beardless throats remains unforgettable.

Harvard was on a wartime footing, the relatively few civilian students either too young for the draft, like myself, or excused for medical reasons. Near me lived a blind student who earned tuition by tuning pianos and two graduate students, one of them black, who fascinated me with their *outré* behavior and outrageous sallies. Both were homosexual—something I perceived only dimly. They soon became good friends and frequent companions. Not once did either of them attempt an advance, though perhaps I was simply too innocent to recognize the moves (a possibility that can by no means be excluded).

My academic career at Harvard started disastrously. I had decided to major in classics, having been told that Greek and Latin were the best preparation for the study of theology. In my freshman year, I failed both subjects and was placed on academic probation. It was my first real taste of failure, made all the more painful by a previous record of uninterrupted success.

What had happened, my father asked. I told him that I was unprepared for the level of work expected at Harvard. My Latin and Greek teachers at school had been amateurs: good men who set high standards in life, but who, in the classroom, may have been only one lesson ahead of their pupils in the textbook. It was not difficult for a bright student like myself to get top marks with only modest effort. At Harvard I was sitting under scholars of world repute.

After the shock of initial failure, I pulled myself together, got off probation, and even onto the honor roll. I accomplished this by prodigious feats of memory at the end of each semester. Starting the afternoon before the final exams, I would read, with a parallel English translation, all the Greek or Latin passages on which we would be examined the next day. I dreaded these all-night cramming sessions. They left me exhausted but able, nonetheless, to recall the passage when I saw it in the examination room only hours later, and thus to produce a fluent and reasonably accurate translation.

I was, however, in constant danger—rather like the legendary horseman who galloped in late winter across the frozen surface of Lake Constance, always inches ahead of the breaking ice. I was simply too young, and too immature, for college. I lacked disciplined study habits. That I survived at all was due to native intelligence and a keen memory, both of them gifts and not achievements.

* * *

Midway through my four years at college the scene changed

radically with the influx of students returning from the war. Not only were they older, they had greater sophistication and experience of life than undergraduates before or since. Harvard, always a stimulating place, was even more exciting than usual in those immediate post-war years.

From the start I had sung in the Harvard Glee Club. The training was outstanding. I would put it to good use years later as director of the Gilbert and Sullivan operetta *Trial by Jury* at the international seminary Canisianum in Innsbruck in 1961 and as founder and director of a German parish choir in Münster in the late 1960s.

The return of the veterans brought an explosion of other musical and dramatic activities. I played Ernest in Oscar Wilde's *The Importance of Being Earnest* and sang the role of Strephon in Gilbert and Sullivan's *Iolanthe.* The most enjoyable of my extra-curricular activities at college were the two Hasty Pudding Club musicals in which I had leading roles. We took both shows on tour as far as Washington and Chicago, staying with alumni and dancing the night away at post-performance parties to the music we had just sung, played by the professional orchestra that traveled with us. In Washington I was lodged, with two others, at the Royal Danish Embassy. Returning inebriated from the party in the wee hours, I slipped at the top of the long flight of marble stairs and rolled, completely relaxed, to the bottom, where I picked myself up, none the worse for the experience.

* * *

Halfway through my college career I had a spring romance with a girl at Radcliffe College (since absorbed into Harvard). It was a heady experience to find that she returned my affection. We parted for the summer with promises to correspond. My letters were more frequent than hers and expressed stronger emotion. Toward the end of the summer, she wrote breaking things off. We met again to return keepsakes we had exchanged. I handled the parting badly—another sign of immaturity.

Within months I met in Portland, Maine, where my father had become Dean of St. Luke's Cathedral in 1945, a seventeen-year-old schoolgirl who captured my heart completely. When she made it clear that she loved me, I could not believe my good fortune.

A cheerful extrovert active in games and sports and easy on the eye, Anne brought me out of myself and gave me a self-confidence I had not previously enjoyed. We wrote each other daily. Every weekend that I could manage, I hitchhiked from Cambridge to Portland to be with her. (My thirty-dollar monthly allowance did not cover paid transportation. For comparison, Harvard's annual undergraduate tuition was then five hundred dollars.) Anne once visited me in Cambridge for a weekend. My father sent me a supplementary check for twenty-five dollars so that we could enjoy ourselves. How wonderfully generous he could be. I wrote him at once to express my gratitude.

About a month into our relationship I told Anne that I wanted to marry her one day. When she said she wanted to marry me, my happiness was complete. We were still sufficiently in touch with reality, however, to realize that matrimony was out of the question for the foreseeable future. We told each other that we would wait.

Not long thereafter my father visited me in Cambridge. I told him how much Anne and I loved each other, that we wanted to marry, but knew we must wait. His delight at my news increased my happiness, which remained undiminished even when he expressed doubt, gently and kindly, that the love of two people so young (seventeen and eighteen respectively) would last. "Something will happen," he told me. My father and I came closer to one another in that conversation than ever before or since.

My father's prognosis proved correct. With no warning at all (at least none that I could perceive), Anne wrote me saying that she was no longer in love with me. I was devastated. My father wrote me a wonderfully sympathetic letter in which he nowhere said, "I told you so." Instead he urged me to throw myself into my work, avoid recriminations, and do what I could to remain Anne's friend. That I largely succeeded in following this advice showed that I had matured since my childish behavior with the Radcliffe girl who had preceded Anne.

I encountered Anne two or three years later with her fiancé. She greeted me with great friendliness and told me that I had taught her a lot. I took this to be a reference to conversations we had had about sex, about which I considered myself, at age eighteen, one of my generation's leading experts. I was too naïve to realize that fully half my Harvard classmates had empirical knowledge of which I was wholly innocent.

* * *

Through all these experiences I never lost sight of the goal of priesthood. I served Mass regularly in the church of the Cowley Fathers (an Anglican religious order) on Memorial Drive in Cambridge, a handsome granite building designed by Ralph Adams Cram, architect also of the gothic nave of the Cathedral of St. John the Divine in New York, where I had spent my childhood. Throughout my undergraduate years I regularly made my confession to an elderly English Cowley Father who represented Anglo-Catholicism at its finest: ascetical, learned, and austere.

From time to time I also visited St. Paul's Catholic Church, across the street from my rooms in Adams House. I found the slapdash liturgical style—the Mass mostly silent, the Latin (when it could be heard at all) so gabbled and garbled that it might as well have been Chinese—off-putting.

I was put off too by encounters with Fr. Leonard Feeney, S.J., who presided over the Catholic student chaplaincy at St. Benedict's Center. In one conversation Father Feeney explained Jesus' response to the rich young man who asked what he must do "to possess everlasting life" (Matthew 19:16). Jesus, Father Feeney told me, gave the man a choice: he could keep the commandments or achieve "treasure in heaven" (vs. 21) by selling all his possessions. To get into heaven, Feeney explained, one needed only to keep the commandments. If one chose, however, one could earn extra points and achieve a higher place in heaven by taking vows of poverty, celibacy, and obedience. I knew no theology at the time, but this double standard sounded fishy to me. (In Feeney's defense, I must note that his exegesis was standard Catholic fare at that time.)

How delighted I was when Vatican II said two decades later that there was but one standard of morality for all: "All the faithful, whatever their condition or state—though each in his own way—are called by the Lord to that perfection of sanctity by which the Father himself is perfect" (*Constitution on the Church*, 11).

When Feeney's literal interpretation of the maxim, "outside the church no salvation" was condemned by the Roman Holy Office in 1949, and Feeney himself was excommunicated four years later for refusing to moderate his teaching, I was not surprised. I had found this leading exponent of Catholicism at Harvard (he had converted a number of undergraduates from Establishment families who had sent their sons to Harvard for generations and persuaded them to enroll at Catholic colleges lest they imperil their immortal souls) even more off-putting than his Church's tacky and formalistic liturgy.

* * *

Having started college when Harvard was on its accelerated wartime schedule, I completed all requirements for the bachelor of arts degree in February 1948, three months before my twentieth birthday. By Commencement Day in June I had already started the study of theology in England. I was not present in the Yard, therefore, when Harvard's president welcomed my classmates "into the company of educated men." (Harvard welcomes recipients of doctors' degrees "into the company of learned men.") I would not attend a Harvard Commencement until my thirty-fifth class reunion in 1983.

8

Kelham

One of my mentors during my college years was Father Gordon B. Wadhams, Rector of the Episcopal Church of the Resurrection on East 74TH Street in Manhattan, an Anglo-Catholic and a gifted preacher. On visits to New York, I would make my confession to him and discuss spiritual topics, including prayer and my desire for priesthood. It was thus natural that I should consult him about seminary training.

My father had not attended seminary. Following graduation from Princeton in 1919, he had "read divinity" at Oxford. He suggested that I do the same. Father Wadhams felt that after four years at Harvard I needed the spiritual discipline of a seminary. A parishioner of his, Walter McVeigh, was studying at the House of the Sacred Mission (run by a men's religious order of that name) at Kelham, in the midlands of England, and had sent back enthusiastic reports. Wadhams suggested that I consider joining McVeigh.[9]

The idea appealed to me. I had been aware of Kelham since

my school years, when I had read *Liturgy and Society* by Fr. Gabriel Hebert, Kelham's leading theologian. Encountered later in the classroom, he proved to be the worst teacher I have ever experienced. His book, however, made a deep impression on me, giving me my first understanding of the centrality of the Eucharist in Christian life and worship. The book contained several pictures of the Kelham chapel, with its massive stone altar beneath a huge archway of brick, topped by a heroic sculpture of a muscular Christ on the Cross, flanked by the figures of Mary and the Beloved Disciple. The pictures had haunted me since my early teens.

To Kelham I applied, therefore, and was accepted. I was told that I could begin my studies after Easter 1948. This fitted nicely with the conclusion of my studies at Harvard in February. On a bitter cold day in March, I boarded a small passenger ship of the Furness-Withy Line for the voyage from Boston to Liverpool. Awaiting me on board were two telegrams. The first was from Dr. Spear, the priest who had given our family such wonderful support at the time of my mother's death:

> May your joys be as deep as the ocean and your troubles as light as its foam.

The second was from a Harvard friend, who wired:

> Congratulations on your success. Contact fat man with garlic breath in A-deck stateroom and follow plan B. In Lisbon our agent is gypsy flamenco dancer with mole below navel in Café Toreador. Exercise caution at all times. See you in Ankara or at any rate Tashkent. Love to Barovna.
>
> Kranf Batoc

The signature was an anagram for Frank Cabot, whose generous friendship and wit continue to enrich my life today.

These messages proved to be the last cheerful note I would experience for some time. The voyage, which I had eagerly anticipated, was grim. The food was an unappetizing foretaste of the conditions then prevailing in England, where food was still rationed. The North Atlantic was stormy. At Liverpool I took the boat train to London, where I found a room in a bed-and-breakfast establishment in Cavendish Square. Having lived away from home, quite happily, from the age of twelve, I was unprepared for the homesickness that overcame me. Alone in the vast metropolis, I was overwhelmed with feelings of desolation and depression. Friends of my father's from his Oxford days entertained me as generously as they could in the prevailing austerity conditions. But nothing could banish my feeling of loneliness and near despair.

* * *

Kelham is three miles distant from Newark-on-Trent, a market town with a fine parish church 120 miles north of London on the Great North Road between the capital and Edinburgh. The Kelham chapel amply fulfilled my expectations: a great square building of brick surmounted by a concrete dome covering the altar and the dramatic rood arch already described. In front of the altar were choir stalls facing each other, separated by a broad expanse of waxed linoleum tiles. When I later suggested that we could save much time and labor by polishing this area, as well as the corridors throughout the adjoining house, with an electric waxing machine rather than with the heavy weighted brushes we pushed to and fro at the end of long poles,

I was told that this appeal to American ideas of efficiency was "against religious poverty."

This principle was invoked to explain much else that astonished me. Here was a community of 120, three miles from the nearest town, without motorized transport of any kind save the ancient motorcycle on which the Steward (a lay brother of the Society) visited Newark for errands. Provisions and other supplies were delivered or fetched in a horse-drawn cart. There was no refrigerator for food. Milk was stored in large steel buckets covered with cheese cloth. In summer it sometimes soured.

The house itself, an ugly neo-gothic pile in red brick three stories high with towers, had been built in the nineteenth century by the famed architect Sir George Gilbert Scott for the Manners-Sutton family, which produced an Archbishop of Canterbury, a Speaker of the House of Commons, and a Lord Chancellor of Ireland.

The large square between the modern chapel and the former main entrance to the house was the original glass-roofed porte-cochere used by horse-drawn carriages. This became the refectory. There we ate off tin plates in silence, to the accompaniment (save at breakfast) of reading from a raised lectern. On feast days we could talk. Since the heating (by antique hot water radiators in the public rooms of the house only and unequal to their task) was regulated by the calendar and not the thermometer, we could often see our breath in the air as we ate.

We slept and studied in three- and four-person rooms heated by coke stoves. The fuel had to be fetched up several flights of stairs, and the ashes carried away in buckets. The stoves always went out overnight and had to be relit in the morning. Our beds consisted of a simple mattress on wooden slats, placed lengthwise atop two saw horses. Next to each bed was a chair and table at which we studied and wrote our assigned weekly essays.

The House Rule (read aloud in chapel at the beginning of each term) required us, on arising, to take a cold shower five times a week. This penance we performed in vast drafty bathrooms with uncurtained stalls. As for the other sanitary facilities, the less said the better. Known universally as *topoi* (plural of the Greek *topos*, "place"), they exemplified the observation of countless American visitors to England: that the people who invented the water closet never perfected it.

We wore dark gray cassocks (save when housework or sports made this impractical), and over the cassock a scapular: a long, rectangular cloth of light blue denim with a hole for the head and falling just below the knees front and back. This helped keep the cassock clean. Absence from the house and grounds required special permission, which was not readily granted.

One wonders how many Catholic seminarians in Western countries today would persevere to ordination if they were required to undergo even a far milder version of this regimen.

* * *

Our formation resembled not so much that provided by pre-Vatican II Catholic seminaries as the novitiate of a male religious order of that era. A religious novitiate lasts only a year, however, or at most two. The Kelham course was four years long. Moreover, we were being formed not as religious but as parish priests. Students were not allowed to become engaged before ordination, but most would marry afterward.

The atmosphere differed from that prevailing in Catholic institutions of that era in two further respects. There was no attempt to shield us from unsuitable reading, lest we "lose our faith." The community received the leading English newspapers and serious periodicals, which were eagerly read. And the only prohibition of "particular friendships" (a major concern in pre-Vatican II Catholic seminaries) was the provision in the House Rule limiting contact with the boys who were completing their secondary education in "the Cottage," a separate wing of the house: "Men shall not form friendships with boys. They shall not go for walks together."

* * *

The academic training at Kelham was mediocre. Of lasting value, however, was the required weekly essay on an assigned topic. The discipline of having to produce, by a Saturday deadline, coherent written reflections on one of the areas of theological study, taken in rotation, was excellent training for sermon preparation later.

I read widely, by choice, in the areas of ascetical and mystical theology: Teresa of Ávila, John of the Cross, Francis de Sales, Abbot Columba Marmion, Sister Elizabeth of the Trinity. It was at Kelham that biography became, as it has remained ever since, my favorite literary genre. I read everything I could find about the Oxford Movement of the 1830s and its leaders, Keble, Newman, and Pusey, who labored to revive Anglicanism's Catholic heritage. I read about the Anglo-Catholics who followed in their wake: Charles Lowder, Vicar of St. Peter's, London Docks, in the 1860s, and his colleague Alexander Mackonochie of St. Alban's, Holborn. I was thrilled by the life of Frank Weston, bishop of Zanzibar, who as president of the Second Anglo-Catholic Congress of 1923 inspired the famous telegram to the pope:

> 1600 Anglo-Catholics, in congress assembled, offer respectful greetings to the Holy Father, humbly praying that the day of peace may quickly break.

I read Trochu's biography of the Curé of Ars, St. John Vianney, and O'Rahilly's life of the remarkable Irish Jesuit, Fr. William Doyle, who flagellated himself with a whip of razor blades, climbed on the altar to embrace the tabernacle, kept careful count of his thousands of ejaculatory prayers, and fell as a British Army chaplain in World War I, venerated by his beloved Tommies, who never dreamed of their padre's bizarre devotional practices.

The Practice of the Presence of God by Brother Lawrence inspired me to emulate this seventeenth-century French ex-soldier and Carmelite lay brother, who remained always recollected as he presided over the kitchen in his Parisian monastery. If he could do it, why not I? Constantly thinking about God was clearly impractical. I decided to recall God's presence during activities that did not require close concentration. Finding the right one proved difficult. After several false starts, I hit on the idea of turning to God whenever I went up or down stairs. After years of perseverance this practice has become habitual—a source of rich blessing and inner joy.

* * *

The book that made the deepest impression on me was *The Soul of the Apostolate* by the French Trappist Abbot Jean-Baptiste Chautard. Originally published in 1910 under the more appropriate title *L'âme du tout apostolat* (The Soul of All Apostolic Work), it has been reissued many times in numerous translations. I reread it a few years back and found it dated.

But its central theme remains timeless: that Christian ministry of any kind is an exercise in futility unless it is firmly rooted in a disciplined life of prayer—not just when one feels like it, but day in and day out, regardless of feelings or whether one "gets anything out of it." Neglect of this fundamental truth is the root cause of much of the Church's present difficulties. Herewith two examples from personal experience.

A few years ago, a fine younger priest described to a clergy gathering his work as Vocation Director. In conversation afterward I suggested that he draw up a simple rule of life for young men considering priesthood. I told him about the rule I had followed during my own high school years, and how it had helped me. This suggestion was clearly unwelcome. "They're not certain about priesthood yet," my colleague told me. How sad. Would not a rule of life, centered on prayer, benefit any young person, quite apart from the question of religious vocation?

The second example is more disturbing still. Some years ago a woman parishioner told me that her son, then a college undergraduate, was thinking about entering the Society of Jesus. I immediately invited him to dinner. Our conversation afterward went on for several hours. He had recently attended a Jesuit Vocation Weekend.

"Were they any talks on prayer?" I inquired.

He told me there were not. I was appalled, but not surprised. How could any religious vocation flourish if it was not rooted in the disciplined practice of prayer? I explained the importance of such a foundation, introduced the young man to mental prayer, explaining the difference between discursive meditation and contemplation, and drew up a rule of life for him. He soaked up all this information like a sponge absorbing water. After his first year as a Jesuit novice, he wrote me that I had done more to nourish his vocation than any Jesuit. It was a joy to attend his ordination to the priesthood some years later.

* * *

I cannot conclude this account of the spiritual formation I received at Kelham without citing liberally from the little book of *Principles* given to each student upon entering.

- By this you were created, the will of God; and to this end, the praise of his glory. If your life is not your own, your time belongs to God. Learn to occupy every moment, and in the best way. Pray, meditate, do some act of charity. The conversation of the brethren should help and cheer us, but God's voice speaks most often in silence. Keep some part of every day free from all noise and the voices of men, for human distraction and craving for it hinder divine peace.
- Do not lament the smallness of your capacities. Such complaints come either of laziness or of affectation or of ambition. Everybody is clever enough for what God wants of him and strong enough for what he is set to do, if not for what he would like to be.
- Choose for yourself the lowest place, not because of modesty, but because it is most fit for you. Remember it is one thing to choose the lowest place, another to be put there. The first may be affectation, but if anyone can take the latter humbly and naturally as his due, such has begun to learn Christ.

- If your work weary you, if it overpass your strength, do it first; you may think about rest afterward. If it cost you your life, what better could you ask than that the time of trial be very short, since the reward is the same?
- Do not be in haste to justify yourself. There are many ways of going wrong, and there may well be many you have overlooked that you need to learn about. Confession and contrition are much better suited to our lips and are of more value than the demonstration of our own virtue.
- In regard to outer things, first it is necessary that you should so exercise yourself in self-mastery that there shall be nothing you cannot easily lay aside. You must learn to leave all one day, whether you will or not.
- Do not think too much about yourself. Your own opinions and feelings may well be of less importance than they seem to you.
- Flee jealousy like fire. Rejoice in another's good, for in him too is the divine good pleasure which alone you seek.
- You may have much to bear, most people have, but it is not well to make everybody bear it. There is always someone whose burden is heavier than yours. Find him out, and if you can, help him.
- Do not despair about yourself, for that has ruined many souls and vocations. God, who is infinite holiness, has borne with you a long time; you may well bear with yourself a little till his grace shall have done its perfect work.

The spirituality expressed in these pithy sentences, some of them Zen-like in their simplicity, made a lasting impression on me. As actually lived in the Kelham community, however, they suffered from a fatal defect. They engendered no joy.

Young people are naturally enthusiastic. They respond generously to the call to sacrifice. Kelham's *Principles* expressed this call eloquently. They needed support, however, from the spirit of joy embodied in Jesus' parables of the buried treasure and the costly pearl (Matthew 13:44–46). This Kelham did not supply.

The atmosphere of the place was aptly captured in an anecdote about the visitor who, upon being shown the chapel, commented: "It looks like a place where human sacrifice is offered."

"It is," came the stark response.

Brother George Every, Kelham's eccentric but enormously learned church historian and also a poet, confirmed this impression in verse:

> This is a place for human sacrifice,
>
> and on that altar stone young men must die.
>
> The green king on the great red mountain
>
> Cries his burden: Crucify
>
> Yourselves, for I am crucified.[10]

My three years at Kelham were shadowed by darkness. The physical austerities described above did not bother me. My root problem was loneliness. My mother's death had left me with a deficit of human affection, which I tried in vain to fill. It would take me decades to learn that the heart's deepest longings can be satisfied only by God.

With my father, 1931

With my mother in Bermuda, 1931

With my father, 1932

At age 5

"The Jay nose: visible in portraits of the Chief Justice, and in the mirror to myself."

Just married! Daddy and Bina following their wedding on May 7th, 1941. Overnight he seemed ten years younger.

I snapped this picture of my father outside the Deanery in Portland, Maine, on Easter Day 1947.

Daddy and Bina, ca. 1950.

With my brother Dudley (left) in the Swiss alps, 1950.

Hugh Astor asked me to be an usher at his wedding in November 1950.

A self-portrait at my priestly ordination, April 3rd, 1954.

Schoolmaster at Collegium Augustinianum, Gasedonck by Goch, 1964.

Preparing to raise sail in Holland.

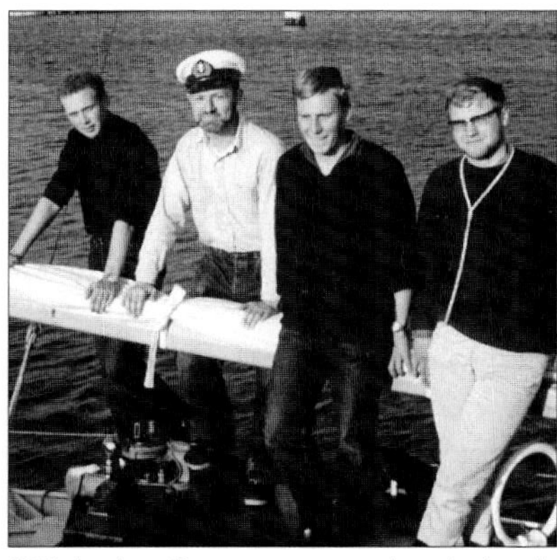

With the German crew that helped me win a Silver Medal from the German Cruising Club for a voyage of 1000+ miles across the North Sea and through the Baltic in 1963.

Cruising down a Dutch canal, 1964,

With Bina in Ireland, 1988.

With my remarkable 89-years-young stepmother on an ocean cruise, 1989.

Bina off Cape Horn, January 1992.

At the Taj Mahal, 1998.

In the fullness of years.

Presenting two of my books to Pope John Paul II, 1995. The photo graced my Christmas card that year, with the caption: "John Paul and I wish you all the blessings of this Holy Season."

"If I were to die tonight, I would die a happy man."

With my father, 1931

With my mother in Bermuda, 1931

With my father, 1932

At age 5

"The Jay nose: visible in portraits of the Chief Justice, and in the mirror to myself."

Just married! Daddy and Bina following their wedding on May 7th, 1941. Overnight he seemed ten years younger.

I snapped this picture of my father outside the Deanery in Portland, Maine, on Easter Day 1947.

Daddy and Bina, ca. 1950.

With my brother Dudley (left) in the Swiss alps, 1950.

Hugh Astor asked me to be an usher at his wedding in November 1950.

A self-portrait at my priestly ordination, April 3rd, 1954.

Schoolmaster at Collegium Augustinianum, Gasedonck by Goch, 1964.

Preparing to raise sail in Holland.

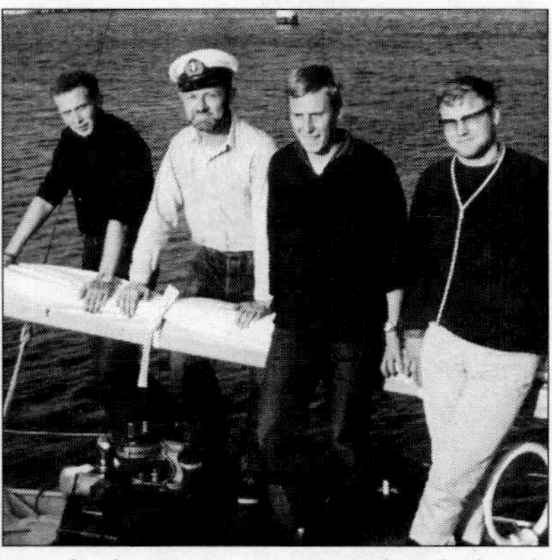

With the German crew that helped me win a Silver Medal from the German Cruising Club for a voyage of 1000+ miles across the North Sea and through the Baltic in 1963.

Cruising down a
Dutch canal, 1964,

With Bina in Ireland, 1988.

With my remarkable 89-
years-young stepmother on
an ocean cruise, 1989.

Bina off Cape Horn,
January 1992.

At the Taj Mahal, 1998.

In the fullness of years.

Presenting two of my books to Pope John Paul II, 1995. The photo graced my Christmas card that year, with the caption: "John Paul and I wish you all the blessings of this Holy Season."

"If I were to die tonight, I would die a happy man."

9

Light in Darkness

Kelham was not unrelieved gloom. There were happy times even there. Standing one day at afternoon tea in a circle of students, one of our teachers, a priest esteemed for his insight and wit, announced: "Jay is like one of those lead-weighted child's dolls; as soon as you knock him down, he bobs up again." He had discerned one of the many gifts bestowed on me by a generous Creator: a cause for thanksgiving then and ever after.

I lived, however, for the vacations. In July 1948 I made the first of many trips to continental Europe, taking with me the four-speed English bicycle that I had acquired on arrival a few months previously. As the Channel steamer from Newhaven entered the harbor of Dieppe, I thrilled at the sight of the life-size crucifix on the breakwater. I was too naïve to realize that France had long since ceased to be a Catholic country. The boat train brought me to Paris, where I found a room in the Hotel des Saints Pères in the street of that name. My father told me later that he had stayed in the same hotel during his Oxford years.

I rode all over Paris on my bicycle: to Notre Dame, the Invalides, the Place de la Concorde, the Arc de Triomphe, the Eiffel Tower, and the ugly Sacré Coeur Church atop Montmartre, with its breathtaking view of one of the world's most beautiful cities. Descending into the Place Pigalle, I halted at mid-afternoon to buy a soft drink from a sidewalk vendor. A young woman, painted and lacquered and wearing a short skirt, approached and brushed against my tropic zone. Unnerved by this first encounter with a person I dimly realized must be a prostitute, I leapt back onto the bicycle and sped off, my heart pumping almost as fast as my legs.

A few days later, I boarded the Orient Express with a second-class ticket to Florence, where I was to visit Tim and Leolyn Spelman, American friends of my stepmother. As we rolled through Switzerland shortly after dawn, an elderly French lady in the crowded compartment extracted from her large embroidered handbag a hardboiled egg, a monogrammed silver spoon, and a salt shaker. Cracking the egg with her spoon, she threw the pieces of shell on the floor and proceeded to eat her breakfast.

At Domodóssola, the Italian border station, I walked back along the station platform to make sure that my precious bicycle was still in the baggage car. I was horrified to see it on the platform, held by a uniformed customs official who was having a screaming argument, in Italian, with a colleague. I hadn't the faintest idea what they were saying, but feared I would never see the bicycle again. Suddenly the clouds lifted; the bicycle was reloaded onto the baggage car, and I returned, greatly relieved, to my compartment.

* * *

My hosts in Florence lived in an 800-year-old villa south of the Arno with a fine view of the city. The house had been commandeered by the Germans during the war. With a combined weight of six hundred pounds, the Spelmans looked like fugitives from a casting call for a Fellini movie. A family story recounted that when Leolyn donated a cast-off pair of slacks to a younger female relative, the recipient had fashioned a skirt from one of the legs. Tim, who had once been slender, had attained his own considerable girth by increasing his intake of food and drink to keep up with his spouse. This entailed abandonment of his career as a pianist. The servants called him "Signor Maestro" in tribute.

Florence was my introduction to Italy. It swept me off my feet. My ground-floor bedroom had a high, barred window overlooking the street. One morning I was awakened by a company of soldiers marching by, singing the Marian hymn *Salve regina* to a rollicking melody. Where but in Italy, I reflected, would such a thing be possible?

Cycling all over Florence, its streets not yet choked by the traffic produced by the economic boom years later, I was surprised by the number of fair-haired youths, so different in appearance from the swarthy, dark-skinned Italians from the poorer south whom I was accustomed to seeing back home. When I asked my hosts about this, they told me it was the result of German incursions centuries earlier.

* * *

The Italian railway brought me, with my bicycle, to Rome, where I found inexpensive lodging in a *pensione* on the Via Veneto—today one of the priciest addresses in one of the most expensive cities in Europe. I was astonished to find how small the ancient city had been. On my bicycle I could ride in twenty minutes from the nearby Porta Pinciana in the northern city wall to the Porta San Sebastiano in the south.

Friends in England had told me it was madness to take the bicycle to impoverished, war-torn Italy. It would be stolen the first day, they said. I always locked the bicycle to a lamppost or railing with a padlock and stout chain. It would have been easy, however, to cut the chain. And in 1948 a good English bicycle was an object of considerable value in Italy. Yet I always found the bicycle where I had left it, even when I returned, past midnight, from a performance of Arrigo Boïto's opera *Mefistofele* in the ruins of the Baths of Caracalla.

Strolling one day through the Pincio Gardens adjacent to the Villa Borghese, I was accosted by a young man seated on a park bench.

"What time is it?" he asked in Italian-accented English.

I told him, and he thanked me.

"Sit down," he said with a distinct lisp.

To what entanglements this was intended as the preliminary, I never learned. Finding both the young man and his invitation off-putting, I continued on my way. He lacked the professional approach of the Parisian lady in the Place Pigalle.

* * *

When my allotted time in Rome was over, I bought a one-way railway ticket north to Ventimiglia, the last town on the Italian Riviera before the French border town of Menton. Continuing westward by bicycle on the Moyenne Corniche (the middle of the three winding roads along the spectacularly beautiful coast), I found myself on the second evening at La Napoule, a few kilometers beyond Cannes. I put up at a modest bed-and-breakfast establishment and sauntered forth in search of dinner. In the town square was an attractive restaurant with outside tables. I normally studied the posted menu to ascertain that the meal would be within my budget: five dollars a day for lodging and three meals. (This was quite possible in 1948, when Europe was still recovering from war and the dollar was king.) There was no menu in sight, only the chef's diploma from the Cordon Bleu cooking school in Paris. Too inexperienced to realize that I was going precipitously upmarket, I sat down at a vacant table.

An attentive waiter recited the evening's offerings, which I followed with difficulty given my limited French. With considerable relief I made out the word *bouillabaisse.* I recalled our French teacher at South Kent telling us that this was a delectable fish stew served in Marseilles. Like a drowning man clutching at a life ring, I told the waiter that I would have the *bouillabaisse*. To precede I ordered pâté and a half-bottle of white wine.

I experienced another moment of panic when the piece of resistance arrived. A *langouste*, the clawless warm-water lobster, was standing bolt upright in the middle of a large soup bowl supported on all sides by seafood of various kinds. Accompanying this intimidating display was a covered soup tureen. I hadn't a clue how I was supposed to deal with these offerings. Seeing my discomfiture, the waiter took pity on me. With a practiced hand he extracted the meat from the *langouste*, removed the debris, and poured some of the soup into the bowl.

To describe the *bouillabaisse* as delicious would be to understate the chef's achievement. It was one of the truly memorable meals of my life. As I ate, expensive cars arrived with elegantly dressed people who gradually filled the tables around me. Still too naïve to realize that I was hopelessly *déclassé* in this exalted company, I continued to enjoy my meal, ordering fruit and cheese in conclusion.

Reality set in when the waiter brought me the bill. It was the equivalent of twenty American dollars—a trifling sum today, but in 1948 enough to feed and house me for four days. Aghast at the sum demanded, I called the waiter to question it, carefully rehearsing the description of my repast beforehand in my best schoolboy French.

"Monsieur, I had only pâté, *bouillabaisse*, fruit, cheese, and a half-bottle of wine. *Est-ce correct?*"

"Oui, Monsieur," he replied, "*parce que les poissons dans la bouillabaisse sont très, très cher. Compris?*

I told him that I did *compris*, and I reached for my wallet. Fortunately it contained just enough to pay the bill. Humbled and unnerved by my extravagance, I realized dimly even then that the meal had been beyond price. Years later the experience helped me to understand the description of the dozen or so restaurants in all France judged worthy of three stars in the *Guide Michelin*: "In a restaurant of this category, price plays no role."

Following stops at Aix-en-Provence and Avignon (where I found a small child on the famous bridge over the swiftly flowing Rhône singing the song I had learned as a child: *Sur le pont, d'Avignon / On y danse, on y danse*), I put the bicycle on the train for Paris. Continuing on by rail and channel steamer to England, I stayed overnight in the Cathedral Close at Canterbury with two elderly ladies, friends of my father's from his Oxford days. Perversely (for I knew that it would offend his deep love of England), I wrote him that returning to England after my glorious month on the continent was "like coming out of the sunshine into the rain." I loved my father dearly. I thrilled at the receipt of every one of his letters. Yet I was often a trial to him.

* * *

My vacation home in England was 35 Chester Row. A small house near Sloane Square, it was the home of a classmate of my mother's at New York's Brearley School, Alexandra Dalziel, the younger sister of Diana Vreeland, in her day high priestess of fashion. Alex, as she was known by her friends, had married a Scottish baronet and become Lady Kinloch. I called her Aunt Alex. Her marriage having ended in divorce, she was living with her daughter Emi-Lu, two years younger than myself and a London debutante when she first walked into my life.

I decided in advance that Emi-Lu would fit my stereotype of English girlhood: hairy-legged, flat-chested, and a rush of teeth to the face. How mistaken can one be? I first glimpsed her in the mirror of the "loo" (toilet) on the landing between that ground floor and upstairs sitting room of her mother's house.

"Jay?" she called out as she came in the front door. I looked down toward the mirror and saw a vision of loveliness coming up the stairs to greet me. I loved her at once. From the start we were like brother and sister. I found Emi-Lu the most naturally good person I have ever known. At a party or dance she would be found talking to a shy wallflower or to some elderly stranger. Trying to convince her that not everyone shared her high standards was an exercise in futility.

My first visit to Chester Row established a pattern, which

never varied. Upon arrival from Newark at King's Cross station, I would take a taxi to Londonderry House in Park Lane, which housed the office of the Royal Aero Club, of which Lady Kinloch was secretary. Until World War II the beautiful building had been a center of political entertaining in London. It has long since disappeared beneath the wrecker's ball, replaced by an undistinguished high-rise tower.

Asking the cabby to wait at the curb, I would run up the great marble staircase, greet Aunt Alex, and get the house key from her. Upon her return later in the day, we would exchange our news and make plans for the days ahead.

These soon came to include parties and visits to country houses to which my friendship with Emi-Lu gave me the entrée. These included a cocktail party with the late Princess Margaret, and many weekends at a lovely country house (now a super-expensive bed-and-breakfast establishment) presided over by Viscountess Hambleden, a lady-in-waiting to Queen Elizabeth, mother of Britain's present queen. On a visit to England in March 1994, I found her obituary in *The Times*. Feeling a rush of gratitude to this noble lady, as handsome as she was good, I said a prayer for the repose of her soul.

On my return from a continental holiday in 1950, Aunt Alex told me, "Emi-Lu is engaged to Hugh Astor"—one of the three Astor brothers, whose father, Lord Astor of Hever, then owned the London *Times.* The brothers later took over the paper themselves. I was happy for Emi-Lu and told her so. I realized, however, that Emi-Lu, once married into the upper echelons of the British Establishment, would be living in a world that was not mine. Hugh asked me to be an usher at his wedding in November 1950—a tribute, I assumed, to his bride. I anticipated that my friendship with Emi-Lu would be reduced to the exchange of Christmas cards. I was wrong once again.

Hugh soon became a good and generous friend. He and Emi-Lu entertained me countless times at Folly Farm, the beautiful country house they soon acquired near Reading. I have seen the couple's three daughters and two sons grow from infancy to marriage and parenthood. On May 14, 1978, Hugh and Emi-Lu gave me a splendid fiftieth birthday party at Folly Farm. Exactly twenty-four years later, Emi-Lu, a widow since Hugh's death in 1999, duplicated this honor with a seventy-fourth birthday party in her elegant flat next to London's Westminster Cathedral. Three of her five children were present, with spouses.

* * *

When the time came for me to leave England in May 1951, Aunt Alex, normally the most unemotional of women, was on the verge of tears. Pausing on the stairs of the Chester Row house, as she went off to work, she told me, with a breaking voice: "Jay, you're the closest thing to a son that I have."

It is the nicest thing anyone has ever said to me.

10

Roman Fever

On October 3, 1950, I wrote my father from Kelham telling him I had recently dreamt that I was celebrating the Catholic Mass in Latin and feeling happy to do so. I told him that the question of whether I should enter "the Roman Church" (as I then called it) was "something I ought to consider seriously before my ordination, but I don't know how to consider it properly."

The dream would prove only half right. Though I would later celebrate Mass in Latin on occasion, it has never appealed to me. My feelings were best expressed by the parish priest with whom I served in Münster for two years at the end of the 1960s. Having been ordained a decade before Vatican II, he had then celebrated Mass far more often in Latin than in the vernacular.

"The Latin goes in here," he said, pointing to his head, "but not in here," indicating his heart. (He was more fortunate than most. An American Jesuit and university professor told me recently: "We never understood many of the prayers we were saying.")

My personal faith in 1950, and for a decade thereafter, could be called "Catholicism without the pope." Deciding whether to enter the pope's church required, therefore, a careful study of the papal claims to infallibility and universal primacy. My Anglican teachers told me that these claims were illegitimate additions to the faith of the ancient church, to which Anglicans appealed as normative.

Lacking the maturity and learning to undertake the requisite study, I framed the question in terms of the existence, or not, of a personal call to leave the church of my baptism. Though I did not know it then, I was following the counsel of the Downside Benedictine, Dom John Chapman, regarding the call to religious life: "I hold that the rule to be followed is this: 'I am not meant to be a religious, unless God *forces* me into it.' In other words, if a man feels 'I must,' then it is a true vocation, and not otherwise."[11]

Like Catholic-minded Anglicans generally, I deplored having to live in a Church that included many whose beliefs, especially about Mass and priesthood, were shaped by Protestant rather than Catholic ideas. I had been taught, however, that such defects were the unavoidable consequence of life in a fallen world. The "pure" church for which I longed did not exist this side of heaven.

The Roman Catholic Church, my mentors pointed out, had its own defects. The most obvious were the papal claims to infallibility and universal jurisdiction, which (as then ceaselessly trumpeted in a flood of popular Catholic polemic) would have been indignantly rejected, I was confident, by such early

Church Fathers as Augustine, Cyprian, and Chrysostom as perversions of the Church's original faith.

Moving from Anglicanism to Rome entailed, therefore, exchanging familiar ecclesial shortcomings for others which, once encountered, would prove equally distressing. The grass always looked greener on the other side of the fence. I was an Anglican not by personal choice, but by divine providence. Abandoning the church in which God had put me, without the certainty of a divine call to do so, would be (so my Anglican mentors told me) "to refuse the Cross."

Compounding the difficulty of resolving this question was my father's attitude. He who could be so generous, whose religion, like mine, was also Catholicism without the pope, was relentlessly harsh in his judgment of an Anglican priest who (as he put it) "abandoned his ordination vows" to become a Roman Catholic. When my erstwhile mentor, Gordon Wadhams, took this step, my father said sternly: "We must never mention his name or have anything more to do with him."

How could he say that? I protested. "Even if we don't agree with him, surely we must respect him for following his conscience."

This appeal to religious liberty was immediately swept aside as unworthy of consideration in the face of incontrovertible evidence of moral collapse: the breaking of a solemn religious oath.

Consistent with this view was my father's use of the term "Roman fever" to designate the condition of an Anglican who was thinking of becoming a Roman Catholic. While this was common Anglican usage at that time, along with such expressions as "swimming the Tiber" and "poping," it was normally devoid of malice. For my father, however, "Roman fever" designated a moral illness of deadly virulence, to be combated as the work of the Evil One himself. Anglican priests who succumbed were, to my father, not converts but "perverts." More than once I heard him say of such reprobates: "He perverted to Rome."

In my father's defense, it should be noted that his attitude differed little from that of many pre-Vatican II Catholics toward Catholic priests who left the priesthood to marry, or to become Protestant ministers.

* * *

The Kelham course was four years long. In the autumn of 1950 I decided to leave at the end of three years and to complete my studies at the General Theological Seminary of the Episcopal Church in New York City. Parish ministry in my own country (my sole expectation then and for years thereafter) required, I felt, at least a year in an American seminary.

In an attempt to resolve my doubts about the Church, I decided to visit Rome for Holy Week and Easter 1951. I found accommodation with the Benedictines at San Girolamo (St. Jerome), a community of mostly Belgian and Luxembourg scholars founded by Pope Pius XI to revise St. Jerome's Latin translation of the Bible (the Vulgate), then still the authentic text for Catholics. I arrived there shortly before Palm Sunday 1951.

Not wishing to disturb my father unnecessarily (since it was entirely possible that I would be able to resolve my doubts in favor of the Church of my baptism), I informed him only about my itinerary, without saying anything about its underlying purpose. This led to bitter accusations of deception and disloyalty when I opened my perplexity to him in a lengthy letter from Rome on Easter Monday.

After saying in this communication that he would doubtlessly have surmised "the real reason I have come to Rome," I said that I wanted "*before* my ordination to face up squarely and absolutely honestly to the claims of the Roman Church and, with God's help, make quite sure that it is as an Anglican and not as a Roman Catholic that God wishes me to serve him."

I told my father about a conversation I had with the English Rector of the Beda College for "late vocations," Monsignor Duchemin. He had made no effort to convert me, but encouraged me to study carefully the issues in dispute between Canterbury and Rome. I had begun, I told my father, "to have a strong feeling that God will one day call me into the Roman Church." I admitted that the grounds for this feeling were meager. My doubts about Anglicanism, I wrote, were "not so much intellectual doubts, as moral ones: Is it really honest for me to be a Catholic [in faith] and yet not be in the Roman Church? Would I really be a loyal Anglican believing (as I do) that only 'Catholic' Anglicans are right and that the 'Liberal' and 'Protestant' ones are wrong?"

There was absolutely no question, I assured my father, of my being converted to the Roman Church on the basis of ten days in Rome. But I was writing now to tell him that he must be prepared for the possibility of my reception into the Roman Church—"I should think within the next year. But I have not yet been 'converted' and I certainly think that I ought not to make any decision until I come home and have a chance to talk to you."

All this, I wrote, had caused me many tears,

because of the pain which I know I would cause you by taking any such step as I have mentioned. Please do not think it would be an easy step for me; you know how eagerly I have looked forward to ordination ever since I was twelve years old. During all my difficulties at Kelham, one of the thoughts that sustained me most was the knowledge that one day I would be a priest and you would be standing beside me at the altar while I said my first Mass. To give up all those hopes would be a very painful thing. But I count this as nothing compared to the pain and disappointment I would be causing you by abandoning the Anglican Communion that we *both* love so well.

Yes, I know you will say that I am not causing you pain (though on the purely human level you won't be able to help feeling at least keen disappointment); that you will rejoice that I'm still trying to serve God, even if you can't agree that the road I've chosen is right; that you're still proud of me, etc. And in a way the knowledge that the news this letter brings will meet with such a generous response from you makes it almost more painful for me to write all this. If I knew that you would disown me for becoming a Roman Catholic, I could simply clench my teeth and "prefer God rather than men." But to know that through everything you will not cease to be the most loving and generous father that anyone could have, and to know that I would in a way be trading on that generosity in joining the Roman Church, this is indeed painful to me.

I wrote that I would always be deeply grateful for all he had taught me by word and deed, especially in religious matters. He had taught me to be a Christian and a Catholic Christian, and I thanked God for that. I hoped and prayed that I would never cease to love the Anglican Communion. And even if I came to see that God was calling me to leave Anglicanism, I recognized that there were many Anglicans who had received no such call and, by God's grace, attained real sanctity as Anglicans.

> Aside from my anxiety on your account, I am at rest mentally and am trying patiently to await whatever outcome God will send, knowing that whatever happens, God will be glorified thereby, and that *whatever* God is preparing for me, it is much more wonderful than anything I could plan or prepare for myself. So I pray for God to make his will known to me and to give me the courage to follow his will without counting the cost. And I know this will be your prayer too. Need I say, Daddy, that I love you now, and all the family, just as much as I ever have. I pray for you every day and always shall. I am only sorry that I am not more worthy of the love that you all have given me. God helping me, I shall always be,
>
> Your loving, devoted, and grateful son.

* * *

The generous response of which I wrote toward the end of this anguished letter (far longer than the summary above indicates) was not forthcoming. Instead I received a cable, "Please start home at once," and a letter of grim foreboding about my "emotional state." Enclosed was a prayer my father had written as a student at Oxford three decades before which, he hoped, "may yet keep you back from the step you are apparently about to take." I thanked him for the prayer, but failed to see its relevance. It touched none of the questions that were troubling me.

By contemplating the possibility of becoming a Roman Catholic, my father wrote, I had ceased to be a candidate for ordination in the Episcopal Church. No Anglican seminary could now admit me as a student. The real decision before me, therefore, was not which Church I would belong to, but whether I intended to become a priest or not.

This characteristically apodictic pronouncement, excluding for reasons never stated (presumably because they were, at least to my father, self-evident) the possibility that I might become a priest in the Catholic Church, would remain a mystery to me until 1994, when I discovered among my letters to my father, which he had preserved, one he had written to me but never sent when my crisis of conscience resumed in 1959–1960.[12]

Letters I wrote to my father from England, following my return from Rome, show my efforts to resolve my doubts, while dealing as best I could with an attitude on my father's side that both magnified my difficulties and caused me deep distress.

On April 7, I wrote asking my father to remember that I was still an Anglican. During my three years at Kelham I had been told repeatedly that I must face up to doubts about my faith. Until now, however, I had no doubts. Now that they had come, I was finally doing what my teachers had told me I must do. How could this make me ineligible for study at an Anglican seminary?

I had not found any Anglican in England, I told my father, who shared his harsh attitude toward an Anglican, even a priest, who becomes a Roman Catholic. When Fr. Gordon Wadhams had taken this step, my father had said that this would entail Wadhams saying that my father had been feeding his people "poison" all these years. The statement had shocked me, I wrote, and I knew it to be untrue.

> An intelligent Roman Catholic would not think of saying such a thing any more than we [Anglicans] would think of saying that the bread and grape juice of a Baptist communion service were "poison." We deny the *validity* of Protestant orders. But "validity" is a very narrow technical term. It is in no sense equal to efficacy.

In response to my father's charge that considering becoming a Roman Catholic was "refusing the Cross," I told him that taking such a step would mean accepting an even heavier cross. I asked him not to add to its weight by talking (as he had done) "of the completely unnecessary and illogical step of resigning your ministry." He had told me years before that his father had been ordained in the Presbyterian Church out of respect for his own father, who was a minister in that church, only to seek Anglican ordination a few years later. I asked my father not to put his own son in a similar position.

One of those I consulted following my return to England was the Bishop of Oxford, Dr. Kenneth Kirk, an Anglo-Catholic and a widely respected scholar. I had often stayed with him during my Kelham years. He had given me much valuable advice and encouragement. I laid my difficulties before him now, first by letter, later in a personal visit. The bishop, I told my father, had confirmed me in the course I had already determined on: to continue my normal life as an Anglican, while investigating the Roman claims with the greatest care, and with as complete objectivity as possible.

There was no question, Dr. Kirk told me, of my doubts rendering me ineligible for study at an Anglican seminary. The only thing to which my doubts were a bar was Anglican ordination. Were I to be refused the opportunity study "the Roman question" in an Anglican institution, I wrote my father, I would have to study it with Roman Catholics as teachers, "and that would probably decide the question in their favor quite rapidly."

I told my father that in a two-hour conversation with Bishop Kirk, we had differed on one point only. He contended that intellectual study, if pursued long enough, could resolve the issues in dispute between Rome and Canterbury. While not disputing the primary importance of intellectual study, I inclined to the view that this alone could never give me the answer I was seeking. "You could go on all your life," I said, "and still not be satisfied that you had covered the whole ground or that there was not something more to be considered."

On May 4, 1951, just ten days before my twenty-third birthday, I boarded an American merchant ship for the voyage home.

II

Coming Home

The day before my birthday I was met at the pier in New York by my Uncle Rowland, the second of my father's three younger brothers. The father of two daughters but no son, he had taken a keen interest in me since my childhood. He was a strikingly handsome man, amusing and full of fun. I was delighted to see him. Over dinner in the University Club, where he entertained me overnight, it became clear from his guarded remarks that he was equally delighted, and not a little surprised, to encounter a cheerful young adult able to converse easily on a variety of topics, rather than the emotional basket case my father had led him to expect.

The reunion with my father in Portland was stiff and awkward. By dallying with "the glamour of Rome" (as he would describe it some years later in a circular letter to relatives, when my crisis of faith recurred), I had come close to disgracing not only myself but the whole family. Storm clouds hovered over us throughout the summer. The intimacy we had enjoyed ever since my mother's death was gone forever.

Only in later years did I come to realize that I had remained, well into my twenties, emotionally dependent on my father to a degree that was neither normal nor healthy. He had told me during my college years that my relationship with my mother was unusually close. When she died, I transferred to him all the intense love I had had for her. Reading decades later—in David McCullough's *Mornings on Horseback* and in H.W. Brands' *T.R., The Last Romantic*—about the young Theodore Roosevelt's devotion to his father, I recognized my attitude toward my own father. I adored him. His talk, especially about ecclesiastical matters, could hold me captive for hours. Even as a schoolboy, I spent hours poring over the books in his extensive library.

This helps explain why, as I have already written, I was never a teenager. Nothing in the adolescent world could possibly rival, for me, the fascination of my father's world. By age twelve I was already a junior adult, able to deal independently with trains, buses, and shopping for personal necessities. This led me to think that I was unusually mature for my age. A school classmate whom I encountered decades after our graduation told me that I was so regarded by my peers as well: "You weren't a boy," he recalled. "You were an adult."

This early maturity in one area concealed underdevelopment in another. Shedding my emotional dependence on my father came late and involved deep pain for both of us.

* * *

In September 1951 I entered the General Theological Seminary of the Episcopal Church in New York City. After reviewing the work I had done at Kelham, where the course was differently structured, the authorities gave me credit for three semesters. I could complete the requirements for the degree in three more. If all went well, I could look forward to ordination as a deacon in 1953 and as priest a year later.

My doubts about the Church were never really resolved. They simply faded away—a process which was greatly assisted by my experience of Catholicism in my own country. My father was mistaken in supposing that I found Roman Catholicism glamorous. On the contrary, I found the pre-Vatican II Church in the United States thoroughly off-putting.

My earliest knowledge of the Catholic Church came through our devoted Irish nurse, Kitty. She came to us while my mother was still living, and remained until my father's remarriage in 1941. I could not have been more than seven when Kitty took me one day to her parish church a few blocks north of our home at the cathedral. A large congregation was reciting the rosary. From the pulpit a priest bawled out (no other expression is adequate to describe the sound that assaulted my youthful ears) the opening words of each petition at breakneck speed. The congregation responded at the same tempo. What struck me most forcefully was the absence of any attempt at common prayer. In place of the reverent unison recitation of public prayers to which I was accustomed in the Episcopal Church, I heard only a cacophony of individual voices, each going as fast as possible. I was appalled.

When, years later, I started to attend Mass in Catholic churches, this childhood impression of a liturgical wasteland was deepened. When I find Catholics today who rhapsodize about the beauty and reverence of the old Latin Mass, I reflect that they must have either short memories or none at all. Only in a Benedictine or Trappist monastery did the pre-Vatican II Mass have dignity, beauty, and that quality—indispensable for good liturgy and widely lamented because of its absence today—mystery.

I have written already about my dislike of the Catholic liturgies I experienced during my Harvard years. More than once I encountered celebrants who were halfway through the vernacular prayers at the end of Mass before my ears registered the shift from Latin to English. An American archbishop told me recently that he was shocked to discover, as a newly ordained priest, that the pastor of the parish to which he was assigned omitted whole parts of the Mass so that he could get through the rite more quickly. An Anglican priest-friend stated it aptly when he remarked, midway during a Holy Week liturgy we were attending in a Catholic cathedral in the American Southwest: "These people have taken all the romance out of Catholicism."

The Catholic clergy I encountered did little to commend their Church to me. I have already described my conversations with the Jesuit Fr. Feeney at Harvard. Unforgotten, because unforgettable, was my encounter with a Catholic bishop, Ordinary of a Midwestern diocese, aboard the steamship *Queen Elizabeth* during my one trip home from Kelham, in the summer of 1949. Before the days of universal air travel, the numerous passenger liners plying the Atlantic carried many Catholic priests on each summer voyage. Since concelebration was then unknown, there were back-to-back Masses each morning in the first-class lounge.

So it was that I found myself one morning attending the bishop's Mass. I made the Latin responses, but did not communicate. Later that day the bishop encountered me on deck and struck up a conversation. He clearly failed to understand my statement that I was an Anglican seminarian, for he asked whether I was in philosophy or theology. I explained that we did not have this division, emphasizing again that I was an Anglican.

"Oh," he responded with obvious displeasure. "But you were answering my Mass."

"Yes," I replied. "Our own Mass is very much like yours. And I know Latin."

"Oh," he snorted angrily and turned immediately on his heel and walked away. I was twenty-one.

During my time at General Seminary, my field education (as it would be called today) involved collecting a small group of pupils once a week from a Manhattan public school and taking them to the local Episcopal church for religious instruction, as permitted under the "Released Time" provision of New York state law. Waiting nearby each week for the considerably larger group of Catholic children was a curate from the local Catholic parish. He always crossed to the other side of the street to avoid contact with a heretic. Several years later, a well-known monsignor in Arizona, where I served from 1956 to 1959, regularly refused to acknowledge a friendly greeting from me or any other Anglican priest.

Our seminary professor of Pastoral Theology warned us not to expect much in the way of dialogue from Catholic clergy. "You will find that after ten minutes at most he has repeated all he can recall from the theological manual he studied at seminary, and the exchange will come to a halt. Now, if you want to talk about baseball, the conversation can go on all afternoon."

I was also troubled, while at General Seminary, by Catholics' lack of interest in the social dimension of the Gospel. The small but costly Catholic Church and rectory across the street from the seminary, which contrasted sharply with the neighborhood's ugly commercial buildings, epitomized this myopia. More than once I saw the pastor entering or leaving a limousine driven by a liveried chauffeur.

The newspapers were full just then of reports about an investigation of corruption and crime, murders included, on the nearby waterfront. A central figure in the investigation was the president of the local longshoremen's union, Tom Ryan, a worshiper at the Catholic Church in question. Questioned about his view of the alleged activities of his controversial parishioner, the pastor replied: "I keep my nose out of Tom Ryan's union, and he keeps his nose out of the affairs of this parish." I found the cynicism embodied in this statement troubling.

Troubling too was the willingness of Catholics of that era to use political clout for institutional advancement, exemplified by prelates like Cardinal O'Connell in Boston and Spellman in New York. This aspect of their history is obscured from the vision of American Catholics by the anti-Catholicism that has been part of American life from colonial days. Andrew Greeley has shown that it remains alive and well today: in the elite universities, the great foundations, and the media.[13]

Episcopal Bishop Horace W.B. Donegan of New York gave a striking example of this political clout in his address to the diocesan convention in May 1953, which I attended as a deacon. After reporting that in the past year he had received 193 adult Catholics into the Episcopal Church, he explained that he mentioned this because of

> the widespread erroneous notion that the traffic is in the other direction. This impression is due principally to the large publicity given to such as go to Rome. For example, when last year a Curate in one of our parishes became a Roman Catholic, many inches of type were devoted to it. But this year, when a distinguished former Roman Catholic priest, a noted scholar and author, a former member of the faculty of the Catholic University of America, was received by me in the Cathedral Church, though all the facts were furnished to all the daily papers, not one line appeared in any of them.[14]

Everyone present knew the reason: editors were unwilling to risk the wrath of Cardinal Spellman. I can still recall the gasp of horror from some five hundred men at this example of naked Catholic power.

12

Reaching the Goal

Catholic power was the last thing on my mind as I completed my studies at General Seminary in the autumn of 1952. Living in an intellectually alive community of fellow believers and studying with better teachers than those I had experienced at Kelham had restored my faith in Anglicanism.

I was fully aware of its shortcomings, about which I have written already. From the start Anglicanism has tolerated, even gloried in, a wide diversity of religious belief. Anglican apologists call this "comprehensiveness" and claim it as a source of strength. To me it was grave weakness. Others might call Anglicanism a big tent. I considered it a house of cards.

But it was *my* house. At its best it was very good. And it was that best that I loved. The teachers who represented the best in Anglicanism were clearly my superiors: intellectually, spiritually, and morally. If they were content to remain Anglicans, who was I to claim that I had found something better? I was conscious of no clear call to forsake the Church of my baptism.

And to move without such a call would be to abandon the post to which God had assigned me through birth and upbringing.

Bishop Donegan of New York consented to ordain me deacon in the Cathedral of St. John the Divine on February 2, 1953. When I wrote this news to my father, inviting him to preach at the ordination (at which I was to be the only candidate), he replied with a characteristically stern letter pointing out that I had never "repudiated the Roman claims," and challenging me to do so before proceeding further.

I replied that my faith was not based on repudiations. All my advisers had told me that it was right to proceed to ordination in the Episcopal Church. Returning to the controversy with Rome would destroy the spiritual equilibrium I had achieved since returning from England—something I was confident my father wanted as little as I. I begged him, therefore, to let sleeping dogs lie and not to press the matter further. To my father's credit, he did not do so.

To be ordained in the New York Cathedral was a privilege and a joy. There I had been baptized in the magnificent octagonal baptistery and font (a picture of which hangs beside me as I write these lines), immediately adjacent to the Chapel of St. Ansgar, where I was to be ordained deacon. My mother's funeral had been held in the Cathedral. There I had first served at the altar, been confirmed by Bishop Manning, and received my First Communion. There I had sung in the choir and learned to play the organ.

My father's sermon contained a reference to my "Roman fever" two years before. In a metaphor so strained that it brought instant smiles to my face and to those of seminary classmates with whom I exchanged knowing glances, he urged me not to emulate the donkey who starved to death tethered between "two succulent bales of hay" through inability to choose which one to eat. Bishop Donegan found the sermon so edifying that he had it published in his diocesan paper.

Midway through the service my half-sister Linden, born seven and a half years previously to my stepmother and father (to their surprised delight and that of the whole family) turned to her mother and asked, "Will we ever see Jay again?"

The equanimity with which the child faced the prospect of never seeing Jay again required deep reserves of manly courage to digest when the question was reported to me after the ceremony.

One of those who shared my amusement at my father's reference to the donkey had been ordained deacon himself just two weeks previously.

"You know, of course, Jay," he remarked to me after the ceremony, "what the charism of the diaconate is."

I confessed that I did not.

"Infallibility," came the immediate reply.

I fear that I displayed more than a little of this quality as a deacon.

* * *

Bishop Donegan waived his right to assign me work in the New York diocese. With his permission I accepted the offer of curacy at Grace Church in Newark, New Jersey, an Anglo-Catholic stronghold in a diocese where such parishes were rare. The church had a fine three-manual organ, a professional choir of boys and men, Sisters who helped with parish visiting and other pastoral ministry, and impeccable liturgy including a sung Mass each

Sunday with deacon and sub-deacon in dalmatics meticulously executing the ceremonial described in Adrian Fortescue's classic and now forgotten work *Ceremonies of the Roman Rite Described.* Supporting all this was a million-dollar endowment—in a day when a million dollars was real money.

Without this financial cushion, the parish could not have survived. The affluent parishioners of yesteryear, whose legacies had built up the endowment, had almost all died. Due to the church's inner-city location, next to City Hall, the congregation was small. Those who still came lived mostly in distant suburbs along with many others whom we never saw, but who remained on the parish register. One of my chief duties was to visit these people in their homes.

Since childhood I had found the excuses offered by the people who refused to attend the banquet in Jesus' parable so far-fetched as to be scarcely credible. The need to inspect recently purchased land or oxen, or being newly married, hardly seemed to me compelling grounds for staying away from a dinner party. (Luke 14:16–20) Parish calls soon taught me that I was mistaken. Though I never asked those I visited whether they still attended Grace Church, my appearance was almost always the cue for the recital of reasons for nonattendance that made the excuses offered by the absentees in Jesus' parable models of self-evident logic.

In most cases the real reason why these people no longer attended the church of which they continued to be registered members was obvious: they lived too far away. A widow in a small walkup apartment, more candid than most, mentioned this and added: "I go to Sacred Heart across the street, Father. It's just about the same."

I gasped. I was well aware of what went on in Sacred Heart Church. To call the hurried, slapdash, mostly silent Masses there "just about the same" as the stately liturgy we celebrated—with beautiful music, gorgeous vestments, flowers, and incense—took my breath away. It also set me thinking. I realized that the liturgy I loved required for its appreciation a level of culture and education which was available to few. For every one like me, there were easily a thousand like that good soul who found the silent Latin Masses at Sacred Heart "just about the same" as the reverent and beautiful liturgies at Grace Church.

Anglicanism, I realized for the first time, was, for all its beauty, not really evangelical. It appealed to the few, not the many. Its beauty continued to hold me captive, however. It would be years before I was able to perceive a truth aptly stated by Newman's biographer, Sheridan Gilley:

> Anglo-Catholicism, the most culturally attractive form of Christianity that I have ever encountered, is bound to be no more than a *preparatio evangelica* to positions more coherent than itself. In its learning, its devotion, its sheer beauty, it is a preparation without equal, but no more.[15]

* * *

Of the parishioners whom we saw regularly at Grace Church, none was more faithful than Miss Cromwell. Standing not five feet tall and weighing, surely, less than a hundred pounds, she wore pince-nez glasses, secured against loss by a tiny gold chain attacked to a hook in her pierced left ear. Miss Cromwell was a daily communicant. Though she lived within easy walking distance of the church, visiting her was problematical. She had such an elaborate program of religious exercises that it was necessary to make an appointment in advance. She was also scrupulous.

One day Miss Cromwell was taken ill. It fell to me to take her to City Hospital in the parish car. On the way I tried to comfort her by assuring her that I would bring her Communion daily.

"Oh, Father," she said, "I won't know what time it is. How can I be sure I am fasting from midnight?"

I told her that such rules did not apply to the sick. I might have been talking to the deaf, for Miss Cromwell's life was guided by rules, and she fretted constantly about breaking one of them, even unknowingly. Hoping to relieve her mind, I told her that even Roman Catholics, who were far stricter about such things than we were, had relaxed the fasting rule. Pope Pius XII had recently shortened the Eucharistic fast to one hour.

"Yes, I read about that," Miss Cromwell said sadly. "And I've prayed that he would change his mind."

The story had an edifying conclusion, however, which taught me a lesson I have never forgotten. Not long after entering hospital, Miss Cromwell had a stroke that impaired her speech. She could say only yes and no. On my daily visits to bring her Communion, I would linger and propose topics for conversation to which she could respond affirmatively or negatively.

"You're thinking about dying, aren't you?" I asked her one day.

"Yes," she replied.

"Well, you're ready to go, aren't you, any time the Lord calls you home?" I asked.

With a beautiful smile and without the slightest hesitation, she replied—her speech momentarily restored: "Why not?"

What a lesson for me! I had judged harshly the narrowness of her religious practice, her false idea of God as a strict judge ever on the watch to punish people for the slightest infraction of his complicated maze of rules. The deficiencies in her faith were obvious. But she had tried far harder, and certainly far longer, than I had. She had done her best. Now, at the end of her life, God let me see how wonderfully good he was to her. The fear that had ruled her life was gone, replaced by childlike trust. She had a happy and a holy death a few days later. I still pray for that dear soul at Mass today. I believe she prays for me.

* * *

The woman who called at the office of Grace Church to arrange her husband's funeral was in a different category entirely. I had not seen her before, nor the daughter, in her early twenties, who accompanied her. They explained that they had little money and were concerned about costs. There was no need to spend a lot of money, I told them. I asked if they would like me to go with them to the funeral home to help make the arrangements and they said they would.

The establishment they had chosen, in a drab part of the city, was called "The People's Burial Company." On the way there I reiterated that it was not necessary to spend a lot of money, and they agreed.

On arrival we were shown into a dingy office furnished with a messy desk, chairs, back issues of *Casket and Sunnyside* (the undertakers' trade paper), and remains of half-smoked cigars in the ash trays. The widow explained that her husband's body was still at City Hospital and that the doctors there wanted to perform an autopsy.

"Ah, nah. You don't want that," the man behind the desk announced. "They just mess around there. I'll call 'em up."

Flicking an ash off his cigar, he picked up the telephone and dialed.

"City Hospital? People's Burial. Gimme the morgue."

He took another pull on his cigar and waited.

"Morgue? People's Burial. Remains of George A. Seals."

Does he expect the remains to come to the telephone? I wondered.

The rest of the conversation was mercifully brief. We settled the time and date for the obsequies. Then it was time for us to be shown into "The Selection Room," containing a display of coffins with price tags that would determine the cost of the funeral. To my dismay the two women immediately rejected the less expensive coffins, which I assured them were quite suitable, and went rapidly upmarket.

"I could help pay for it with my wages," the daughter told her mother. Casting aside their resolutions of economy, they settled on something clearly beyond their means. That was another lesson for me. Most of the good advice in the world is wasted. People will do what they want to do.

My education continued at the funeral two days later. The chief mourner, I observed, was not the widow but a younger woman. She sat apart from mother and daughter. They did not speak.

* * *

Bishop Benjamin Washburn of Newark, no Anglo-Catholic but a true man of God who believed firmly all the articles of the Apostles' and Nicene Creeds, agreed to ordain me to the priesthood in Grace Church on April 3, 1954, the Saturday before what was then called "Passion Sunday." (Decades later I would discover that on the same day Archbishop (later Cardinal) Joseph Ritter of St. Louis had ordained a group of priests in his cathedral. Graciously, they have invited me to join their class.)

I prepared by a private retreat at the beautiful Episcopal Monastery of the Holy Cross overlooking the Hudson River from its west bank. I made my confession to a monk I knew from his visits to South Kent when I was a schoolboy there: Father Alan Whittemore, a man of shining goodness and deep sanctity. When I had finished my sorry tale of sin, he spoke words I have never forgotten: "You're taking a tremendous gamble offering your life to God as a priest. And God is taking an even bigger gamble accepting you. You're just going to trust one another."

The happiness of my ordination day was marred only by my father's inability to share my joy to the full. The reason remained unspoken. But I knew what it was. I had never repudiated the Roman claims. I was saddened too that my father could not stay to stand beside me as I celebrated my first Mass the next day. I accepted, however, that he had to be back in Maine for his own Sunday duties at the Portland Cathedral.

To my great joy, my brother Dudley served at the Mass. Afterward I was so happy that I recited the whole of the long *Te Deum* ("We praise you, O God ... ") aloud in the sacristy.

I had reached my goal. Celebrating Mass that day was wonderful. It is, if possible, even more wonderful today.

13
Parish Priest

Had anyone told me, on the day of my priestly ordination, that I would one day be a university professor and author, I would have dismissed the suggestion out of hand. The only university professors I knew were my teachers at Harvard. I was clearly not in their league.

Parish ministry was the limit of my horizon, and of my ambition. With the impatience of youth I was certain, however, that I could do the job better than the longsuffering rector under whom I served in Newark. He bore with my impetuosity and occasional arrogance with what I now recognize was exemplary patience and charity. He cannot have been greatly distressed when I told him, after two years, that I was ready to move on.

Catholics, familiar with a quasi-military system in which clergy receive assignments from their superiors, have difficulty understanding a clerical body which, though similarly structured, operates quite differently. Unless he belongs to a religious order, a Catholic priest normally serves for life in the diocese for which he was ordained, moving to greater responsibilities on the basis of seniority. Episcopalian clergy compete for positions in a kind of free-market system, moving freely from one diocese to another.

Through an ad in a church paper, I obtained a supply position at the Episcopal Church in Bozeman, Montana, where the rector was taking a two-month sabbatical. I drove there at the end of May 1955 in the first automobile of my own, a used car purchased for $1200 at the time I resigned my curacy in Newark. It was my first experience of the American West.

I had a wonderful time. Since I had Sunday duties only, I was able to visit the national parks promoted by my fellow Harvard graduate Theodore Roosevelt: Yellowstone, the Grand Tetons, and Glacier National Park.

In the autumn I had still not found a parish of my own. Through the good offices of a mentor on the General Seminary faculty, I was offered a curacy at Grace Church in Utica, New York—an example of the informal Old Boy Network operating among the clergy of the Episcopal Church. Like Grace Church in Newark, this was an inner-city church with a congregation mostly from the suburbs. It differed in what Anglicans call "churchmanship," being more "central" than the Anglo-Catholic parish I had served in Newark. The rector, with a fine wife and three children, was a local boy from "the wrong side of the tracks." Offered the rectorship when he was the parish curate and still in his thirties, he had hesitated to accept, thinking the job beyond him. He told me about phoning Dean Fosbroke of General Seminary, where he had studied, for advice.

"Take it, Stan," came the immediate response. "You'll never get another chance like this." He followed this counsel and had done well.

From him I learned a valuable lesson. At a meeting of the parish Vestry (similar to a Catholic Parish Council, but with decision-making authority), the members failed to approve a proposal by the rector. Sharing his disappointment, I asked him afterward why they had not supported him.

"We have to remember, Jay," he told me, "that these men have business and professional relationships which we don't always know about. Some of them who would like to support us aren't always free to do so because of obligations to others." (There were then no women on vestries.)

The second thing I learned during my four months in Utica merits a section of its own.

* * *

My service in Utica coincided with a capital fund drive for renovation of the church plant. This introduced me to an idea that would change my life: the concept of stewardship. Often considered simply a euphemism for fundraising, stewardship, I learned, actually describes a whole way of life, based on the biblical doctrine of creation.

In the second creation tale in Genesis, the man whom God places in Eden is not its owner. The garden belongs to God. God placed man ("Adam" in Hebrew) in the garden "to till it and care for it" (Genesis 2:15). Man was God's agent, his steward, to tend the garden on behalf of its creator and owner. As long as man obeyed the creator's law, he enjoyed the garden's fruits. When man broke God's law, he was expelled from

Eden—the symbol, in Genesis, of the ordered, beautiful world of God's making, in contrast to the disorder and ugliness of human marring.

In terms simple enough for a child to understand, the Genesis creation tale proclaims what the modern ecology movement has rediscovered: that there is a sacred order in nature. When we respect nature's laws, the earth and humankind prosper. When we violate the natural order, we pay a price. We are in this world not as masters, but as servants. We are creation's stewards, accountable to God, our creator.

During that autumn of 1955 in Utica, I learned about "the three T's" of stewardship: time, talent, and treasure. These are gifts entrusted to us by God, for a limited time. Few of us have a century. One day we shall have to give an account to God of how we have used our gifts. Crucial to the right use of these gifts is gratitude to their giver.

Hebrew religion taught the offering of firstfruits. The Jewish farmer and shepherd offered God the first fruits of field and flock, out of gratitude, in recognition that everything comes ultimately from God. Jesus, who learned this practice in childhood from his mother, from St. Joseph, and in the synagogue school at Nazareth, would be shocked to find many of his present-day followers offering God not the firstfruits but leavings: what is left over after they have provided themselves and their loved ones with necessities, and often with many luxuries besides.

This simple message challenged me. I decided to begin the biblical practice of tithing: to return to God voluntarily, out of gratitude, the first ten pennies of every dollar that came to me, from any source. I divided my gifts between church and charities. Contrary to expectation, I found that tithing was not difficult. It was easy. What was left over after giving God "his share" was enough, and more than enough, for all my needs.

Tithing, I found, brought unexpected blessings. Since it is based on faith (trusting that our needs will be taken care of if we give away the first portion of our income), it deepens faith. It enables us to use money sacramentally, by making something material a vehicle of the spiritual—gratitude. And it changes money from a source of worry into a source of joy. After I started to tithe, I discovered, to my delighted surprise, that God can never be outdone in generosity.

Twice in my subsequent life my income would be cut so drastically that I considered suspending my tithe until my finances improved. This happened first when I entered the Catholic Church and had to become a student again before returning to priestly ministry. Over a decade later I found myself unemployed and without a salary for seven years. During both these periods I continued tithing—though my gifts, like my income, were of necessity sharply reduced. I reasoned that I had made a promise to the Lord. He would take care of me.

He always has. Indeed I marvel at the material blessings I have enjoyed on slender financial foundations. In 1977, after more than three years of unemployment, I submitted a sample of my handwriting to a graphologist. One passage in the analysis interested me especially:

> You are not particularly thrifty; your plans for conservation and use of money may be somewhat haphazard. But you are certainly not worrying about money, for your debt frustration is one of the lowest I have ever seen.

I smiled broadly when I read that. On my fiftieth birthday, though still without employment or prospects, I decided that tithing had brought me so many benefits—even material ones—that for as many more years as the Lord gave me I would return to the Lord the first twenty pennies of every dollar he gave me. Reflecting on how tithing has enriched my life, I can say truly: I can't afford to stop.

* * *

Within a few months of my arrival in Utica, the Old Boy Network came through for me again. A fellow alumnus of General Seminary suggested my name to the Vestry of St. John's Episcopal Church in Bisbee, Arizona, his former parish, which was then vacant and looking for a rector. I went out to see and be seen. The Vestry issued the call, and the bishop gave his reluctant consent.

His reluctance was based on a difference in churchmanship. The bishop considered himself an evangelical. In reality more of a liberal Protestant, he was understandably uneasy at accepting into his diocese (territorially large but small in numbers of clergy and laypeople) another Anglo-Catholic like the priest who had recommended me to Bisbee.

I arrived there in February 1956. Located in the mountains of southeastern Arizona just a few miles from the Mexican border, the town was a mile high. Winter brought occasional light snow, which normally melted by noon. Summer days were hot but dry, with most nights cool enough to sleep under a blanket. It was my first experience of the desert Southwest. I quickly discovered that the locals' boast of "an ideal climate" was true.

We never said, "I hope it's a good day tomorrow." The weather was always good. The sun shone and shone.

Mild colorblindness, inherited from my maternal grandfather, prevented me from seeing the subtle desert colors that draw so many artists to the American Southwest. Though I missed, at first, the lush green of my native Northeast, I soon came to appreciate the beauty of the desert, especially the mountains and sunsets.

Bisbee was then an active mining town, owned lock, stock, and barrel by the Phelps Dodge Copper Company. Proud of its Wild West past, it boasted colorfully named streets: Brewery Gulch, Opera Drive, OK Street. The houses were built on hillsides so steep that many were accessible only by long flights of steps. Mail had to be fetched from the post office, since no letter carriers could be found willing to undertake home delivery.

On the single highway leading past the post office toward the Mexican border was an enormous open-pit mine. Trucks as big as a house traversed the terraced roads of the pit day and night, transporting the ore-bearing rock scooped up by gigantic power shovels.

St. John's was not one of the Episcopal Church's more flourishing works. With a congregation that scarcely exceeded a hundred even at Christmas and Easter, and a long history of internecine strife, the parish had been served by thirty rectors in the fifty-odd years of its existence. I knew this record when the position was offered to me. I was impressed, however, with the enthusiasm of the parishioners who interviewed me on my visit. I reflected that the only direction the parish could go was up. I welcomed the challenge.

Within weeks of my arrival I proposed to the Vestry a financial campaign based on the principles of stewardship described above. Despite initial skepticism, and resistance amounting to hostility in some quarters, it was a runaway success. We exceeded our goal by 30%.

My triumphal chariot was off to a good start. But Vengeance came limping after in the form of revived infighting. Part of the trouble was due to my youth and inexperience. (I was, after all, only twenty-seven.) Part was due to a difficulty with which I continued to wrestle for decades: how to deal with reactions (ranging from discomfort through resentment to outright hostility) of ordinary folk to someone they experience as "different."

* * *

I have described already the impression made on me by Abbot Chautard's classic work *The Soul of the Apostolate.* Acting on the lesson he had taught me, I adopted, soon after my arrival in Bisbee, a regimen of personal prayer to which I tried to be faithful through my three years in the parish. Rising early, I would drive the scant mile from my modest house to the church for a half hour of prayer: Morning Prayer ("Matins") from the Anglican Book of Common Prayer and a twenty-minute meditation. For this I used books such as the *Spiritual Exercises* of St. Ignatius Loyola and *The Lord* by Romano Guardini. I would read a brief passage, reflect on it, and make acts of faith, repentance, and thanksgiving. I would learn later that I was practicing what the monks call *lectio divina.* It was a kind of discursive meditation, the only form of mental prayer then known to me. Meditation as usually understood today—emptying the mind of thoughts and images in order to enter into the passive silence of contemplation—was still labeled in books on prayer as suitable for "advanced souls" only. This clearly excluded me.

Once or twice a week I celebrated a weekday Mass. My flock was too small to support anything more. The Mass would follow the personal prayer described above. After this prayer in church, I would return home for breakfast.

* * *

Another priority was preaching. A Protestant work, *Planning a Year's Pulpit Work* by Andrew Watterson Blackwood showed me the importance of long-term planning. Without that, the preacher would ride his hobby horses, preaching on topics that happened to appeal to him and neglecting others of equal or greater importance, because he found them difficult.

I drew up a list of subjects I thought people should hear about at least once a year, dividing them into categories: doctrine, biblical exegesis, moral teaching, pastoral encouragement. Then I turned to the Sunday readings (then the same every year: today's three-year cycle of readings was still far distant). I assigned each of the topics on my list to a specific Sunday. Thus I knew, a year in advance, my sermon topic for each of the next fifty-two Sundays.

I would begin my sermon preparation on Monday, writing down every thought, however insignificant, which the week's readings and topic suggested to me. I then turned to my large and growing personal library. (Theological books could then be bought for a song from antiquarian booksellers in England. I was a regular customer.) From biblical commentaries and other works I gleaned further material. This too I committed to writing in the form of notes.

By midweek I started on the all-important sermon outline. This always started with a short but complete sentence stating as succinctly as possible the sermon's *aim*. What chance was there that the hearers would understand what I was trying to achieve if I could not state it clearly myself? Stating the aim also helped me to eliminate material which, however important in itself, did not further the aim of that particular sermon. It would be saved for a more suitable occasion.

The outline itself always began with an introduction. This might be a question, an arresting quotation, or a reference to a topic of current interest. The object was to construct a "hook" to provoke interest and secure the hearers' attention. The body of the outline normally contained three main points. There might be subheadings within each of these main divisions. At the end of each I always constructed a link to the next section: always a complete sentence. This ensured that the flow of ideas was logical and clear.

As important as the introduction was the sermon's conclusion. I always strove for something positive, challenging, and strong. If the hearers remembered nothing else, they should remember this.

I avoided moralism like the plague. The hearers, I reasoned, were there voluntarily. More than exhortations to be good, they needed reassurance that God loved them despite their failures. The strongest and best motive to continue striving despite these failures, I was convinced, was the gift of God's unconditional love. When I did preach the moral law, I presented it not as the standard we must meet before God would love and bless us, but rather as the description of our grateful response to the blessings and love bestowed on us by our loving heavenly

Father as a free gift—not because we were good enough, but because God was so good that he wanted to share his love with us.

The sermon outline, begun at midweek and revised many times as fresh thoughts came to me, was complete by Saturday morning at the latest. Thereafter the sermon almost wrote itself. I never went into the pulpit without a full manuscript. But I was sufficiently familiar with the text, having read it over aloud to myself at least once, that in delivering it I appeared to be speaking freely, rather than reading.

On the wall next to the desk where I prepared my sermons were quotations from two Anglican preachers: Dean Inge and Canon V.A. Demant, both of St. Paul's Cathedral in London. A quarter century later I would use them to introduce the first of my three volumes of published homilies, *Proclaiming the Good News*:

> The gospel was not good advice but good news. (Dean Inge)
>
> Tell people only what they must do, and you will numb them into despair; you will turn the gospel into a shabby replica of the world's irreligious moralism, with its oceanfulls of good advice. But tell them what they are, of their dignity as made in the image of God, and that their sins are wicked perversions of their nature; tell them that the world with all its horrors is still God's world, though its true order is upside down; tell them that they can do all things through Christ, because in him all the powers of their nature are directed to fruition—and you will help to revive hope in this dispirited generation. (Canon Demant)

* * *

In December 1994 I received a letter from a lawyer in Los Angeles who wrote:

> You do not remember me, but I vividly recall you. About thirty-five years ago, you trained me as an acolyte at St. John's Episcopal Church in Bisbee. I am enclosing a photograph of the two of us, which was taken in front of St. John's just before Sunday Mass in 1958, when I was in the fourth grade. I am now happily married. I am the father of four wonderful children and I too am now a Catholic. I cannot imagine holding any other faith.
>
> My Dad always said you were one of the finest speakers he had ever heard. Public speaking was an interest of his and he had a good ear for it. Even today, whenever your name comes up, Dad usually reminds everyone that he went a whole year without missing a single Sunday Mass while you were at St. John's because he found your sermons to be so helpful.

Such letters are rare—and a good thing too. The Lord in his wisdom does not allow his priests to see most of the good we do, lest we become too conceited. In his mercy he conceals from us most of the harm we do (by our failures, our compromises, our betrayals of the Gospel and of our high calling), lest we become too discouraged.

* * *

I left Bisbee in February 1959, almost three years to the day from the time I arrived. How I came to do so, and where I was bound, requires a fresh chapter.

14

THE CALL OF THE CLOISTER

I had always assumed that I would marry and have children. In preparation I had taken out life insurance shortly after ordination, assuming that I would need it once I had a family, and that it would be good to start at an early age, when the premiums were lower. (Upon becoming a Catholic I suspended the policy. When I became a Catholic priest, I cashed it in. No one will suffer financially from my death. A few people may suffer emotionally. I fear that they will recover faster than I care to contemplate.)

In a letter to my father from January 1957, when I had been in Bisbee a year, I told him that I found the prospect of marriage receding.

> Somehow in the last few months God seems to have shown me that my present way of life is in no sense incomplete. I do not feel either the need or the desire for anything more than the love and strength that God himself gives me through my priesthood.

I was praying, I told my father, that by the time I was thirty (sixteen months hence) God would show me whether he wished me to embrace a celibate vocation. If so, I intended "to regularize my state through an annual vow in connection with one of the religious orders."

The hope of divine guidance by the time I was thirty remained unfulfilled. A God who observes timetables is a human construct—in biblical language an idol—not the God of Abraham, Moses, and Jesus. To resolve matters, I decided to use my three-week vacation in July 1958 for a visit to the small community of Anglican Benedictines at Three Rivers, Michigan.

Toward the end of the visit I wrote my father that for the first week I had found the life tedious and had thought of leaving. After a talk with the Prior, however, I had resolved to stay on for the full three weeks. On a subsequent evening the Prior had given a talk to me and two other aspirants on the Prologue to St. Benedict's Rule, with which I was already familiar.

> Listening to it, I felt like the two disciples on the Emmaus road: my heart burned within me (Luke 24:32). The Prior spoke of how St. Benedict addressed himself to anyone at all—to the average person without any special gifts—who would listen and return to God by the labor of obedience, the God from whom we have all departed by disobedience; of how the monk seeks to repair the disorder of the world not by changing the world, but by changing himself.
>
> To the man who had not seen the Benedictine vision, it was a life of dull and petty routine; but for the monk

> with that vision, every detail, even the smallest and most irksome, brought him into contact with God. The sense of the immediacy of God's presence, once seen, was the thrilling secret of the monk.

As I listened to his words, everything seemed to fall into place, and I felt that I could see, for the first time in my life, what the religious life was really all about and why men entered it—because it led them straight to God.

> We had gone out from this talk to Compline, I told my father, and sometime between then and the time I went to bed, I had decided to be a Benedictine.
>
> So there it is. I have nailed my colors to the mast and I shall not strike them unless and until God gives me a conviction that I should not persevere that is at least as strong as the conviction I now have that I should. I am resolved that mere discouragement shall not make me turn back.

Before my departure a few days later, it was settled that I would return the following summer to test my vocation.

* * *

Unlike Peter, James, and John, who immediately left their nets and boat at Jesus' call to follow him, I decided that it would be nice to have a final trip to Europe before immuring myself behind monastery walls. Old World travel was still unbelievably cheap (by today's standards). I had been saving money toward such a trip for some time. I would make it a monastic pilgrimage, visiting as many monasteries as possible.

On my return to Bisbee, I resumed parish work, telling no

one of the decision I had made until the annual meeting of the parish in January 1959. Then I told the parishioners of my decision to embrace a monastic vocation. It was a privilege, I said, for a priest to serve anywhere. It had been a privilege for me to have served them for the past three years. I thanked them for innumerable acts of kindness and asked forgiveness of anyone I had offended, and of the whole parish for not having served them better.

There was, I said, only one indispensable man: Christ Jesus. If a priest came to think of himself as indispensable, or if his people came to regard him in that light, they were both wrong and it was time for him to move on. A priest's work was to attach people to Jesus Christ, not to himself. He must work in the spirit of St. John the Baptist, who said of Jesus: "He must increase, I must decrease" (John 3:30).

Celebrating my final Mass in the parish on February 22, the Second Sunday in Lent 1959, I preached on the text: "Jesus Christ, the same yesterday, today, yes and forever" (Hebrews 13:8). I spoke of the changes older members of the congregation had seen in the life of the parish. My departure was another change—a small event for the parish, larger in my own life—that was so much shorter and less important than the life of the parish. Change was exciting, I told them, but also sad, for every change reminded us, though we might not realize it, of the great change that awaited every one of us one day, when we must leave everyone and everything we had known and loved and go home, at God's call, to him.

How could we cope with changes so baffling that they sometimes seemed to threaten to sweep away all that we had known and held dear? Only, I said, by finding something unchanging to hang onto. That really was what all of us wanted: something that never changed. And the only thing, the only person in all the universe who never changed was Jesus Christ, "the same yesterday, today, yes and forever." To know and to love him was to be in touch with the one permanent element in a world in which everything else was passing away.

I addressed the concern of parishioners who had told me that shutting myself away in a monastery was a waste of my talents and abilities.

> Let me assure you that the reverse is true. Nothing that is offered to God is ever wasted. From the human point of view, there was never a greater or more sinful waste than the death of Jesus Christ at the premature age of thirty-three. Though he could foresee clearly the end that awaited him, he chose not to stray for a moment from the path his Father had marked out for him. And in the end he threw away his life, with all its rich gifts, with a recklessness and a nobility so great that from that day to this no one has ever dared to pity him.
>
> And what has been the result? Had Christ listened to his friends, taken the precautions they urged upon him, and so managed to live out a normal lifespan, he would have died greatly mourned, no doubt, and beloved by all who had known him. He would have taken an honored place, undoubtedly the chief place, among the world's greatest saints. He would have remained, however, a figure from the past, a man who left behind him a beautiful memory, but nothing more.

By freely offering his life on the Cross, I continued, Christ had made it possible for his Father to raise him to a new life, beyond death. Christ was no dead hero from the past, but a living and present Savior: worshiped the world over, present in the Blessed Sacrament of his body and blood on thousands of altars every day, adored by angels and saints in heaven.

I concluded with a passage on the Eucharist that cited some words of a man who would figure prominently a decade later in my first book, *Absolutely Null and Utterly Void*:

> Remember that it is the altar, where our Lord Jesus Christ dwells continually in the tabernacle, that is the heart and center of the parish. Some thirty years ago a distinguished member of the Church of England, Lord Halifax, whose son was his country's ambassador to our country during World War II, wrote toward the end of his life of ninety years: "As I look back, I see that it is the Blessed Sacrament to which I owe everything. It has helped me in all my temptations; it has kept me, so far as I could have been kept, straight, as nothing else could. Teach our people what the Blessed Sacrament is, and the battle of the faith is largely won."
>
> Make the Blessed Sacrament the heart and soul of your whole life. It will help you in all your temptations; it will keep you straight as nothing else can. Because in a future in which the one certainty is change, and in which you may at times fear that you yourself are being swept away in the rush, the Blessed Sacrament will keep you close to him who never changes; to him whose uniform I am proud to wear, though I wear it unworthily; to him whom I am happy to serve, though

> I fail him every day; to him who loves you more than you can ever imagine: "Jesus Christ, the same yesterday, today, yes and forever."

* * *

I had no inkling, as I preached that sermon, that little more than a year later I would leave the Episcopal Church for the Roman Catholic Church. The sermon is evidence, however, that I was a Catholic in faith long before my shift of ecclesial allegiance. My church I would change; my religion, never.

15

A Monastic Pilgrimage

The journal of my European trip, written on a portable typewriter that I took with me for this purpose, runs to 285 typed pages. Starting in England I drove, in a Volkswagen Beetle ordered in advance and delivered in London, to France, Spain, Italy as far south as Monte Cassino, Switzerland, Austria, Germany, and the Low Countries. The story is best told through excerpts from the pages I wrote on the ship that brought me home.

July 24, 1959: at sea

> And so the trip is over. From the eleventh of March, when I landed in England, until the nineteenth of July, when I sailed from Rotterdam, I spent 129 days in Europe. Of these only twelve were spent in hotels. I have been thirty-seven nights with friends, and six nights have been spent in Roman Catholic hostels of one kind or another. The rest of the time I have been in

monasteries—twenty-three of them Benedictine. And I must have visited at least a dozen other monasteries in addition to those I have actually stayed in. If I say that I have visited fifty religious houses, I shall not be far off.

Save for the Protestant community at Taizé, where I spent two nights, and my visits to Kelham and Nashdom [the Anglican Benedictine abbey in England that founded the Priory at Three Rivers, which I intended to enter], these religious houses have all been Roman Catholic. For three and a half months, I have practically lived off the Roman Catholic Church. I have stayed in its monasteries, eaten its food, slept in its beds, and had my laundry washed by its Sisters. (For any number of times when I asked, in monasteries, where I could get hot water to wash some clothes, they said: "Oh, Father, the Sisters do that.")[16] Some people might say that now the only decent thing to do is to join the Roman Catholic Church myself. I fear, however, that it is not quite so simple as that.

Save for a few days of illness, I have been full of energy and enthusiasm. I have covered over 11,000 miles by car. I return in perfect health and in excellent spirits. It is certainly, from every point of view, the best trip I have ever taken.

The most impressive thing about the trip is to have seen the Holy Spirit at work in the Church, and in the world. The old order is passing away—most obviously, of course, in politics and society, but in the Church as well. We live in an age that is changing with almost breathless rapidity. It is impossible to discern the future, but surely it will be very different from the past, even from the recent past. The Church is slower to change than the world around it. But the Church too is changing.

It is this process that I have been privileged to glimpse on this trip. I have seen Christendom in ferment: the ecumenical movement, the liturgical movement, the revival of religious life among Protestants—these and many other movements of renewal and reform too numerous to list or classify are all signs and symptoms of this ferment... It is obvious, of course, that it is chiefly the Roman Catholic Church that I have seen on this trip, though contacts at Taizé, Geneva [where I had visited the World Council of Churches[17]], and in England have brought me into touch with other parts of Christendom as well. I have seen the Roman Catholic Church at its best. And the best is very good indeed... And yet I cannot honestly say, even after all that I have seen, that I can discern within me any desire to be a part of the Roman Church as it is today. Certainly I have gained from this trip a longing, deeper than any I have had before, for the visible unity of the Church and a corresponding sense of the tragedy of the present divisions between Christians that wound the Body of Christ and drain off its lifeblood.

I bring back not only a written record of my experiences, but a host of memories too: of Bec, the first night I was on the Continent, with its soft air, sweet with the smell of wood smoke, an atmosphere of deep peace, the guest master saying to me as we walked in the garden after supper, "Many people come here seeking this peace"; of Montserrat, with its choir of over a hundred monks, walking in slowly, each one utterly recollected, concentrating on the business at hand, the *opus Dei*[18]; the look of awed reverence on the thin, ascetic face of the young monk there at Montserrat who said Mass for the choir boys, rapt before the sacred mysteries.

Memories too of Lourdes: the long line of sick on their stretchers, each a little bundle of suffering and hope—and faith; pilgrims kneeling on the pavement in the rain at five thirty in the morning for Mass, obeying the Lord's command to "Do this, in remembrance of me."

Memories of monks and monasteries—the smell of hot olive oil in Spanish monasteries, the intensity of the spiritual atmosphere at La Pierre-qui-Vire, the look of utter peace on the faces of that crowd of monks, so many of them young; of Beuron, half a world from St. Gregory's [at Three Rivers, Michigan], yet so much the same.

Memories too of all the monks I have met: old monks, young monks, middle-aged monks; fervent and pious monks, laughing monks, silent monks, solemn monks;

> monks who could sing like angels, and others who could not. I have seen them all and enjoyed them all, and sometimes they have amused me, and often they have interested me, and occasionally they have fascinated me.
>
> But most of all they have edified me and made me want to be a monk like them, like the very best I have met. For I know now, more surely than before I set out, that the monk's life is the most wonderful and the most worthwhile life a man can live here on this earth.
>
> And at the end of all, I have a memory of an ugly little brick church on a side street in Rotterdam and two nuns kneeling motionless before the altar, where the Blessed Sacrament was exposed in a monstrance—and I made my farewell to the Old World and to all these memories, and tried too (but failed) to find some way to tell the Lord how grateful I was for his goodness and generosity and love.

* * *

The monastic vocation about which I was so confident remained unfulfilled. Though I would live with the Benedictines at Three Rivers through the autumn of 1959 and beyond, my uncertainties about the Church (to be described in the next chapter) made it impossible for me to enter the community. After becoming a Roman Catholic at Easter 1960, I visited the Benedictines at Portsmouth, Rhode Island, to enquire about entrance there. The Prior, Dom Aelred Graham, told me on the basis of a single conversation that I had no vocation.

In 1988 my Capuchin spiritual director urged me to try again. I told him that no community would take a man of sixty. He disagreed. With the assistance of Abbot Luke Rigby in St. Louis, a close friend of many years, I applied to the Abbot of St. John's in Collegeville, Minnesota, the largest Benedictine community in North America. He told me on the telephone that I was too old.[19]

My fondness for the monks remains. I was touched and deeply grateful when the St. Louis Benedictines recently made me a Confrater of their community, an honor usually reserved for their major benefactors. For many years I have chosen Benedictine and Trappist monasteries for my annual retreat. I recognize that the *Spiritual Exercises* of St. Ignatius have helped countless souls on the spiritual journey. But Ignatian spirituality is not my scene.

Not long ago a priest from a modern religious order, who was visiting the parish I serve for the annual missionary appeal, said in the sacristy following the Mass I had celebrated, "You're a monk."

No, I told him, I was a diocesan priest.

"The way you celebrated the liturgy made me sure you were a Benedictine," he replied.

He could not have paid me a higher compliment.[20]

16

Apostolic Faith or Catholic Church?

The system in which we have been placed is God's voice for us, till He supersede it. (John Henry Newman)

"Catholicism is a deep matter—you cannot take it up in a teacup."

As for Newman's own reasons for becoming a Catholic, "You cannot buy them for a crown piece"—in fact, "You cannot get them, except at the cost of some portion of the trouble I have been at myself."[21]

For years before my European trip in 1959, I had observed the Roman Catholic Church with an intensity that would have astonished its members if they had been aware of this scrutiny. What I saw, in the United States especially, made me happier every passing month and year to be an Anglican. This attitude began to erode during my monastic pilgrimage.

A conversation with two English Catholics—one a Benedictine monk, the other a seminarian—at the Catholic University of Louvain in Belgium, initiated the change. Finding that they too disliked many of the aspects of Catholicism that I found objectionable, I told them that I considered myself a Catholic already. What made it impossible for me to join their Church, I explained, were the papal claims to primacy (the pope as universal bishop, with all other bishops papal functionaries rather than chief shepherds of their local churches) and to infallibility.

Every Roman Catholic church I entered, I told these new friends, displayed in its tract rack numerous publications arguing that non-Catholic Christians were floundering in uncertainty, advancing mutually conflicting claims that left people confused about what to believe. Catholics, this popular apologetic contended, possessed in Rome an infallible voice that gave the answer to every question.

If Christ intended his Church to have this kind of oracular infallibility, I asked my two friends, why did he not exercise it himself? When people came to him with specific questions—"Who is my neighbor?" "Shall we pay the tax to Caesar or not?" "On what authority do you do these things?"—Jesus avoided the precise, direct answers his questioners sought. Instead he would enunciate a principle, illustrate it with a story or a saying, or ask a counter-question—and then send his questioners off to work things out for themselves. If any of the ancient Church Fathers could see what the pope had become, I contended, they would reject his claim to oracular infallibility as firmly as I did.

"But that's not what we believe at all," my friends responded.

"Well that's certainly the line you're putting out back where I come from," I told them.

This evoked condescending remarks, typical of European intellectuals of that era, about the lack of theological sophistication in the New World.

What then, I asked, did Catholics believe?

The answer I received was unlike any explanation of papal infallibility I had ever encountered. The pope, they assured me, was certainly no oracle. He possessed, according to the definition of the First Vatican Council in 1870, not so much a personal infallibility as the infallibility of the Church. Even this he exercised only under narrowly defined, and correspondingly rare, circumstances. The nature of this infallibility had never been precisely defined, and was left, therefore, to the free speculation of theologians.

The best theologians agreed that infallibility was essentially negative—not inspiration but protection from error. Papal definitions were not necessarily the last word. Indeed, given the limitations of human language, there could never be, strictly speaking, a "last word" in matters of faith, apart from Jesus himself as Word of God—the Father's personal communication to us. The truths of faith would always require restatement as language and patterns of thought changed, and insight deepened. In a given case, it might have been better for a pope to have said nothing, or to have expressed himself differently. But on the rare occasions when he articulated the Church's faith as its official and supreme teacher, at least he would not be wrong.

To these statements, so different from any account of Catholic teaching I had previously heard, I listened with a mixture of astonishment and disbelief. If this was really what the Roman Catholic Church taught, it sounded very much like what I believed already—or at least could believe after a certain amount of study and reflection. But was this really what the Catholic Church taught?[22] It seemed far more likely that I was listening to the view of a small *avant-garde.* If so, it could be only a matter of time before the pope condemned this explanation of Catholic belief in terms as severe as those used by Pius XII in his 1950 encyclical *Humani generis*, which had criticized the *nouvelle théologie* proposed by some of his best theologians in France.

This conversation started me on an investigation of the papal claims that would absorb much of my energies for the better part of a year. For fully ten agonizing months the question of the Church, and of my own conscientious duty, was not out of my waking thoughts for two hours together. I got off lightly. The English "Cowley Father" B. W. Maturin, who became a Roman Catholic in 1897 and drowned in 1915 in the sinking of the *Lusitania* after giving away his life jacket, wrote in his book *The Price of Unity* (1912) that he was on the cross of theological indecision for ten years. After he came into the Catholic Church, Catholic priests with no inkling of his ordeal reproached him for "waiting too long" to join them.

Lifelong Catholics have no notion—can have no notion—of the agonizing struggle confronting an Anglican priest who comes to believe that, in conscience, he must consider moving from Canterbury to Rome. Quite apart from the difficult and complex theological issues (which are by no means as simple and clear-cut as most Catholics assume), there is the need to abandon the oath of loyalty and obedience taken by Anglican priests (as by their Catholic counterparts) at priestly ordination. To do so, the priest is told by his Anglican mentors, would be gravely sinful—a "refusal to carry the cross." Colleagues and friends warn their tormented brother of the potentially grave spiritual harm to those to whom he has ministered and who, with his defection to a body that denies the validity of his every priestly act, find their Christian faith undermined and themselves abandoned by a spiritual guide whom they have trusted and revered. Add to all this the strain, resulting often in total rupture, of personal and family ties of affection and love, and the cup of anguish is full to the brim.

* * *

Though I was unable to address properly the theological issues during the monastic pilgrimage described in the previous chapter, something I read during that trip confirmed the contention of my two friends in Louvain that my understanding of Catholic teaching might be skewed. In 1949 the English Benedictine Aelred Graham, mentioned near the end of the previous chapter, had written:

> Let no one persuade himself that the Catholic position is clearly understood, and that all that remains is for it to be accepted *in toto*. That position at the theological level has not even been stated in English in a manner acceptable to scholars.[23]

If that were true, there was all the more reason for me to investigate what the Catholic position really was.

I began the investigation in August 1959 at a convent in Grand

Rapids, Michigan, assisted by a young American Dominican I had met in Europe, himself a convert from Calvinism. At the end of the month I asked him to receive me into the Roman Catholic Church. Unwilling to make the fierce "Abjuration of Error" then required of converts, which almost implied that one had been in bad faith, I recited the "Emergency Form," which said simply that I accepted all that the Catholic Church taught and condemned what it condemned.

I acted prematurely. The greatest folly of my life? Would that it were. It fully justified the title of this book nonetheless. In heart and mind I was an Anglican still. In September I moved to the Benedictine Priory at Three Rivers, Michigan, living there as a guest in a kind of ecclesial no-man's-land, while continuing my still unfinished task of study, reflection, and prayer.

My research covered three areas: the historical evidence for and against the papacy, Vatican I's definition of papal infallibility, and the history of the English Reformation. I found the historical evidence inconclusive. Opponents of the papacy had overstated their case. But so, clearly, had the papacy's defenders. Of this overstatement on the Catholic side, I give a single example: the case of Pope Honorius (625–638).

Called upon to adjudicate a doctrinal dispute in the Eastern Church as to whether Christ had one will or two, Honorius got it wrong. When opponents pointed out his error, he repeated it. In 680 the Sixth General Council, meeting at Constantinople, formally anathematized Honorius. Pope Leo II ratified the anathema in 682. For centuries newly elected popes were required to affirm the condemnation of Honorius' teaching.

In time the memory of this papal heresy faded in the West,

but was recovered in the fifteenth century. Protestant Reformers cited it against the papacy in the century following. The heresy of Honorius was a major weapon in the armory of the opponents of papal infallibility at Vatican I. It figures prominently in the refutation of the papal claims by Anglican authors. Clearly, if even one pope, speaking *ex cathedra* on a matter of faith (as required by the Vatican I definition), has erred, the doctrine of papal infallibility falls to the ground.

I started my study of this case by consulting a three-volume manual then in common use as a textbook at Catholic seminaries, *Dogmatic Theology* by G.C. van Noort. Honorius, van Noort contended, had not spoken *ex cathedra*. He had merely written a private letter. It was not even certain that he was heretical, merely "a helper of heresy." (Why then, I wondered, the solemn condemnations of the man and his teaching by a general council and subsequent popes?) Some scholars (not many, van Noort admitted) believed that the heretical statements might have been interpolations and not genuine.

Unsatisfied with this superficial treatment, I turned to the lengthy article on Honorius (34 columns of fine print) in the *Dictionnaire de théologie catholique.* Here I found myself in a different world. Flatly contradicting every one of van Noort's arguments, the author admitted that no reputable scholar believed that Honorius had spoken in a purely private capacity, or that his pronouncement was orthodox. After examining the case with meticulous care, the author managed to save the Vatican I definition, but only by means of some fine and careful distinctions that were worlds removed from the facile explanation of van Noort.

The details of the controversy are tedious and have long

since ceased to interest me. At the time, I was satisfied that a crucial argument against papal infallibility had been refuted to my satisfaction. I remained disturbed, however, that the author of a widely used seminary textbook was unwilling to face the difficulty frankly; more, that he claimed it was not really a difficulty at all.

Philip Hughes' three-volume *History of the English Reformation* convinced me that much of the Anglican apologetic with which I was familiar was special pleading. But the historical evidence set forth in the pages of my learned namesake (an Englishman and no relation) neither proved the claims of the pope's Church today nor convinced me that I must be in it.

More and more, it came down to the question of the papal claims, in particular infallibility. The explanation of this (for me) crucial doctrine given to me by my friends in Louvain six months previously was persuasive. But was it authentically Catholic? According to most of the Catholic works then available in English, it was not. To act on the basis of what was, at best, a minority view—and one, moreover, then regarded (as far as I could discover) by most Catholic authorities as suspect, if not flatly heretical—would mean adding folly to folly.

Was communion with the bishop of Rome a necessity (as claimed by members of his Church)? Or was it merely something desirable that his overblown modern claims rendered impossible (as I had believed hitherto)? Entering the pope's Church entailed (as I wrote in the lengthy notes I compiled during this period of agonizing reappraisal and still possess) acceptance of four propositions:

- Christ conferred on Peter primacy over his fellow apostles, and so over the Church.
- This primacy was transmitted to his successors.
- These successors are the bishops of Rome.
- This primacy involved the absolute supremacy in governing and infallible teaching claimed by the pope today, as expounded by Catholic theologians.

I could accept the first three propositions. I considered the fourth an illegitimate addition to the faith of the ancient Church. I was wrestling with the same issues that had confronted John Henry Newman more than a century before:

> The Anglican disputant took his stand upon Antiquity or Apostolicity, the Roman upon Catholicity. The Anglican said to the Roman: "There is but One Faith, the Ancient, and you have not kept to it;" the Roman retorted: "There is but One Church, the Catholic, and you are out of it." ... The cause lay thus, Apostolicity *versus* Catholicity.[24]

17

A Decision

A torment at least equal to that of the struggle for doctrinal clarity was the knowledge that a decision in favor of Rome would deeply wound my beloved father. Six years previously he had been removed from his position as Dean of St. Luke's Cathedral in Portland, Maine. This humiliation—due in part to his imprudence and lack of tact, but a cruel injustice nonetheless—had hurt him deeply. He made light of it, even jested about it. Underneath, however, we who loved him could see the hurt and the bitterness. How, I asked myself many times over in these months, could I possibly inflict this fresh blow on my dear old father?

The passage of time had not softened the harsh attitude he had displayed during my first bout of "Roman fever" in 1951. If anything, my father's views had hardened. The fact that I was now an Anglican priest meant that if I were to become a Roman Catholic, I would be an apostate. I would be joining a Church that (in that pre-ecumenical age) lost no opportunity to declare his priesthood and mine to be invalid; that in its popular apologetic constantly rubbed Anglican noses in the mud, taunted them for belonging to a sham Church that dispensed bogus sacraments, and urged them to join the only body that offered the genuine article. Like it or not, I would be consenting, my father constantly reiterated, to the charge that he was feeding the people to whom he ministered "poison." In conscience, he told me, he could not have such a person in his house.

In letter after letter I pleaded that such an attitude was quite unnecessary, a violation not only of charity but of good sense. None of these appeals was successful. A stand based not upon hurt feelings, but on principle and conscience, cannot be easily abandoned. The story is best told in the letters I wrote him from St. Gregory's Priory in Michigan.

September 9, 1959

Dear Daddy:

Many thanks for your two letters and the messages of reassurance and encouragement they contain. You have always been so good to me, and since I have grown to manhood and moved about the world and met all kinds of people, I have had many, many occasions to thank God for giving me such a father as you are, for I have discovered that most people have not been as blessed in this respect as I. I promise that I shall try my very best always to be a good son to you, and to act upon the principles of loyalty to truth, which you have taught me. We have not always agreed in the past as to just where the truth lies. It may be that we shall differ in this regard in the future. But I want you to know, that having learned first of all from you to love the truth, I shall go on all my life trying to do so, as God reveals more and more of his truth to me... I am in for a difficult time. But you will realize even better than I that there is nothing in my present situation that is incompatible with sanctity. I have the opportunity of daily renewing my faith in God's providence when it is terribly difficult to do so (and without his grace impossible), because the future is a complete blank. In doing this I cannot fail to grow spiritually... So pray for me daily that my faith will not fail, even for an instant. I am naturally full of anxieties about the future. I deal with these on the spiritual level by prayer, consisting mostly of forced acts of trust in God, and on the natural level by discussing these anxieties with the doctor. [I was visiting a psychiatrist weekly, seeking help with the stress I was undergoing.] One of my greatest anxieties is that if I find myself no longer able to agree with your theological position, you will cut me off, hurting both yourself and me in a way too terrible to contemplate.

I pledge you that I shall always respect your theological position and that if in the end I should find myself compelled in conscience to differ from you on some points, this would do nothing to affect my total devotion to you and to all the family. My love for you, and my respect for you, go on no matter what. If I could have some kind of assurance of the same kind from you, it would help me immensely.

Once before, when I was trying to consider my religious position, you threatened me with exile from the family if I could not see things your way. That hurt me more than I can say, Daddy, and I think it has a lot to do with my present difficulties. I do hope and pray that we can both put that completely behind us and go on in the calm assurance that neither of us will ever allow anything at all to destroy the affection and respect we have for each other.

Of course his love for me would continue, my father replied. Death did not terminate love. He still loved my mother. It was several weeks before I replied.

October 2, 1959

Dear Daddy:

I hope that you have not been puzzled or hurt by the fact that I have been so long in replying. I have not wanted to reply hastily to the letter in which you stated your attitude in the eventuality of my entering the Roman Church, and since receiving your letter I have been pondering it and praying over the whole matter.

Let me say that the whole question of my religious future is certainly *not* settled. Clearly, God having made me an Anglican, it is my duty to stay where he has put me unless and until I am morally certain that he wants me to move… There are some things that I want to

> suggest very humbly for your consideration. First, the priesthood is my "pearl of great price." I have never had a single moment's doubt about the validity of your priestly acts or my own, nor about the validity of any of the sacraments I have received as an Anglican. The idea of my ever "denying" any of this (as you suggest) is utterly repugnant to me, and I cannot conceive that I could ever do such a thing... I am impressed by your statement: "One of the best things that Bina and I have is the realization that our life together does not require, or even imply, the repudiation of what has gone before for each of us." [A reference to their previous spouses, both deceased.] May I suggest very humbly that this very principle can be applied, and should be applied, to the case of an Anglican priest who, after long consideration and prayer, was convinced that it was God's will for him to leave the Anglican Church and enter the Roman Church... You are right: nothing good in the past should ever be repudiated. With you, I grieve over the narrow kind of convert to Rome who does repudiate his past. But is it necessary to take that line? Why could one not try to emulate the example of the greatest convert of all time, St. Paul, who in becoming a Christian never repudiated his Judaism, but rejoiced in it to the end?

Why was it, I asked, that none of the Anglican priests I had consulted, starting with Bishop Kirk of Oxford eight years previously (to whom I had gone at my father's urgent request) had agreed with Daddy? Most had expressed doubt that his statements to me could be serious. He welcomed charitable contact with Roman Catholics. Why was his attitude toward his own son so different? To love one another across the barriers which divide us, and in spite of the contradictions of our conflicting claims, was difficult. But it must be done if there was to be any hope of Christian reunion—and it *was* being done all over the world, with the encouragement of the reigning Pope John XXIII.

* * *

To my father, things were seldom what they seemed. Surface appearances hid complex realities beneath. He excelled in the art of *interpretation*. Once launched upon that sea, there was no telling where he would make his landfall. I found a notable example in the second part of the response he wrote, but never sent. I discovered it some thirty-five years later, enclosed with my letter to him from October 2, 1959. On the envelope he had written, "This reply to Jay's letter is not being sent to him at present."

6 October 1959

Dear Jay,

Let me try to answer your letter of October 2, as directly as I can. To do so, I must write not only of my own reasons for making the decision I must with regard to a member of my immediate family who enters the Roman ministry, but also of what I believe to be your state of mind and difficulty at the present time.

My necessity to separate myself entirely from you if you are ordained a Roman priest is not a sign of any end of my love for you as my son; nor is it a judgment on your state of mind or attitude or belief in so doing. It is entirely my judgment on the definition of what you do—and by implication of what you have been, and what I am, as an Anglican priest—by the Roman bishop.

When you submit to Rome you will be baptized; you will be given your "First Communion"; you will be ordained *de novo*. Whether you repudiate what has gone before makes a difference, I suppose, as to the sincerity and frankness with which you are acting. But it makes no difference at all as to the attitude of the bishop who ordains you. He ordains you because you have not yet had the priesthood of the Catholic Church, and he requires you to give public testimony of your assent to that contention by your submitting yourself to his hand.

If your cousin Peter Chase [a Catholic monk and priest at Portsmouth Abbey, Rhode Island] were to submit himself to the [Episcopalian] Bishop of Rhode Island, he would not be baptized or confirmed or ordained. To do any of these to him that have already been done would be a grievous scandal.

When you can shew me [*sic*] that your submission to the [Catholic] Bishop of Providence will be on the same basis, I can assure that I will have neither need nor right to give expression of my feelings by any separation in family relationship... But my opinion

> is that you are not in reality concerned with Roman claims or specially drawn to Rome...I still feel, as I have told you before, that your answer to the call to the ministry has been an unwilling one, and your present distress of mind is due to that conflict. It is complicated by feeling that you are unable to shed, or break, an attitude of subservience to me, inherited from the days of your childhood.
>
> I do not believe that your submission to Rome will help you here. If the yoke of priesthood galls, it will gall still when shaped in the Roman pattern. Even to say *ex animo* that you have never had it on you, and are now putting it on, is not likely to help. And as a Roman, you are still my son, and are even now protesting that my formal ignoring of that fact would be intolerable.
>
> Because of this complication of our relationship I cannot be of help to you at present, but must leave you so far as possible alone. So I do not send you this letter but, having written it in fairness to you and to myself, I put it by in case at some future time it appears right that you should know I have written it just now.
>
> With all my love,
>
> D.

My letters to him in the months following show my continuing personal crisis. My life at St. Gregory's was mostly solitary, I wrote on November 3. It was "just a question of plodding on from day to day, hoping that one day the clouds will begin to lift." On December 26, the twenty-fifth anniversary of my mother's death, I wrote accepting that it was clearly useless for me to attempt further explanations of my situation. Writing a month later, during the Week of Prayer for Christian Unity, I said that God had given me the grace simply to accept the suffering of the ordeal I was passing through, "and with this has come a deep interior peace, and even the beginnings of joy."

This proved temporary, for in early March I mentioned temptations to suicide. To resolve my doubts, I needed "to sit down with a competent Roman Catholic theologian and receive specific answers to a number of questions that I have never been able to settle in my mind." Arrangements were all but complete for me to do this at the Trappist Abbey of St. Joseph in Spencer, Massachusetts. As far as my emotions were concerned, I assured my father, they were all on the side of Anglicanism. "I know the Roman Church well, and it appalls and repels me, especially in its American manifestation. But that, of course, has nothing to do with the matter of truth, which must be judged objectively and rationally, and on the basis of the evidence—not on the basis of what one likes or dislikes emotionally."

The Trappists received me warmly at Spencer, where I was helped during my three-week stay by Fr. Raphael Simon, a fifty-one-year-old Jewish convert and former psychiatrist who had been an intern at New York's Bellevue Hospital during my childhood. I spent a few days, during my stay, with the Jesuits at nearby Weston College seeking help with dogmatic questions. I wrote my father from there on April 9: "My time here has been very profitable, and I find that many theological questions that have puzzled me for years have been solved."

I was nearing a decision. My study of Church history had persuaded me that my Anglican forebears in the sixteenth century had stumbled into schism. There was no need to assign blame, and there was clearly plenty to go around. But having recognized that I was the heir of that schism, it was incumbent upon me to do something about it.

I found myself confronted, as an Anglican priest, by the question put to Jesus by his critics: "By what authority do you do these things?" (Mark 11:28). I had no answer. I realized that I could not, in conscience, remain in the Anglican Church. Once my doubts and misunderstandings about Catholic teaching had been completely removed, I had to act on my convictions, however difficult that might be.

Completely removed? No, that is an overstatement. To the end I had nothing more than moral certainty. How could I be sure that the papacy, in practice, was not (as Anglicans claimed) the negation of episcopacy? That Catholic bishops were no more than papal functionaries, with the pope in reality not merely the universal but sole bishop? How could I know that the explanation of papal infallibility given me by my friends in Louvain a year previously was authentically Catholic, and not the pope-as-oracle doctrine still being trumpeted in triumphalist apologetics?

On none of these questions did I ever achieve complete certainty. I just had to make an act of faith—based upon reason, but not provable on rational grounds alone—that my hesitations and doubts had been resolved. Another convert, the late Monsignor Ronald Knox, wrote once: "In the end the convert is faced with just one question. The Church says: 'Look into my eyes. Do you trust me?' All else is irrelevant."

* * *

One difficulty still held me back: the need to abandon—with no guarantee that it would ever be given back to me—the exercise of the priestly ministry to which I had aspired consciously and without interruption from the age of twelve, and which I had exercised unworthily, but with great joy, for six years. Even if the Roman Catholic Church found me qualified for priesthood, this would involve re-ordination. I did not see how I could ever submit to something that would involve denial of the very thing that had brought me to the threshold of the Catholic Church: the sacraments I had received, and administered myself, in the Anglican Church.

The previous September I had drawn up a document tracing the Table of Consecration of the two Episcopalian bishops who had ordained me deacon and priest respectively. This showed that both could trace their own orders, through co-consecrators, to Old Catholic and Polish National Catholic bishops acknowledged by Rome to be validly ordained.[25] Through the good offices of a Benedictine Prior in Rome who had helped me during my visit there in 1959, I had submitted this document to the Holy Office (now the Congregation for the Doctrine of the Faith), requesting a judgment about the validity of my Anglican orders.

I received a reply in French, on the letterhead *Suprema Congregatio S. Officii*, dated 30 October 1959 and signed "P. Paul Philippe, O.P., Commissaire du Saint-Office." (He later became a cardinal.) The crucial paragraph stated:

> There can be no question of a simple recognition of the orders received, with subsequent permission to

> exercise the priesthood. The church can only require a certain period of studies, at the end of which conditional reordination would be granted; but there is no reason why this would be refused, provided the other conditions mentioned [the normal criteria for ordination] were satisfied.[26]

This was more than I had dared hope for. I put the letter away, hoping that it might one day prove decisive with the Catholic bishop willing to ordain me. I also communicated the substance of this letter to my father, hoping it might soften his attitude. It did not.

I was fully aware, however, that the letter might well prove to be a check that could not be cashed. During my conversations with Father Raphael at Spencer, I discussed the difficulty of abandoning my priesthood, possibly forever.

"Jay," he said to me one day, "why don't you just give your priesthood to Our Lady, asking her to keep it for you, and to give it back to you when the time is right?"

I told him I would like to do this. We knelt down and prayed the Hail Mary three times with this intention.

* * *

On Good Friday, which fell in 1960 on April 15, I wrote my father that I had finally reached a decision. I had been able to resolve my doubts in favor of the Roman Catholic Church. My method had been to take the most convincing anti-Roman arguments I could find, arrange them logically, analyze them—and then see what could be said in reply from the Roman side. In case after case I had seen anti-Roman arguments that previously convinced me crumble under this analysis.

I had not stopped at intellectual study, however. For the past nine months, I wrote, I had spent never less than an hour daily praying for God's guidance, on most days several times that. As far as possible I had tried to free myself from emotion—something I had found difficult, since I had inherited my father's ardent emotional nature. It was not so much that I had come to find Anglicanism wrong, I wrote, as incomplete. I had come to see that the Roman Church was the home of all truth, I told my father, "including Anglican truth, which I first learned from you, and which I shall treasure always." Since it would clearly be dishonest to continue in the ministry of the Episcopal Church believing as I now did, I had written to my bishop in Arizona [still my ecclesiastical superior] telling him that I must in conscience take the painful step of leaving that ministry and entering the Roman Catholic Church.

> I want you to know that *I have not been re-baptized*, conditionally or otherwise. I have not made the customary long Profession of Faith, since it contains some rather harsh statements condemning one's previous faith. Rather I have made a very brief and entirely positive Profession, specially adapted to my circumstances and conscientious convictions, stating simply that "having been brought up in the Anglican Communion, but now by God's grace brought to a fuller knowledge of God's truth," I believe everything that the Roman Catholic Church teaches.

It was specifically understood, I wrote, that I did not deny my priesthood or any of the graces I had received through Anglican sacraments. I would always be grateful for my life as an Anglican. I was simply adding Roman Catholicism on top of it, as St. Paul added Christianity on top of his Judaism. Had I followed my own wishes and emotions, the decision would have gone the other way. I expected a much more difficult life in the Roman Church than I ever had as an Episcopalian—with this important exception, that I would be living on the basis of the whole truth. God had said of St. Paul at his conversion, "I will show him what great things he must suffer for my name's sake" (Acts 9:16). I anticipated something similar myself.

I enumerated the Anglican friends and mentors I had visited to tell them of my decision. Bishop Washburn of Newark, who had ordained me to the priesthood, had commended me for my courage and honesty, wished me well, and had given me his blessing. Sister Mary Regina, an Anglican nun in Peekskill of shining goodness and genuine sanctity, had also told me she admired my courage.[27] The priest who had preached at my priestly ordination told me on the telephone that he "had no answers" to my difficulties. A priest-friend of my father's at the Episcopalian seminary in New Haven, Connecticut, had confirmed that it would be dishonest for me to continue in the Episcopal Church. I had even talked to a former Norbertine abbot who had made the reverse journey. While I respected his decision, I had not found the reasons he gave for it convincing. I assured my father that there would be nothing in any newspaper, religious or secular.[28]

* * *

On Easter Monday, three days after mailing that letter to my father, I was conditionally confirmed by an auxiliary bishop of Boston, busy interring the unburied dead of Holy Week.[29]

I drove the same afternoon to Newport to see my father and Bina (as I had promised in the conclusion of my letter), and to pick up some personal belongings I had left in his rectory.

There was an ugly scene.

"You are *not* welcome in this house," my father told me with all the vehemence at his command.

I tried to reason with him, as I had repeatedly by correspondence. I had not denied his priesthood or my own, I assured him. My Catholic confirmation that very morning had been conditional.

"Is that bishop willing to have that published in the newspaper?" my father demanded angrily.

"*I* am not willing to have it published," I retorted.

In a last desperate attempt to effect a change in his attitude, I pointed out that he was more upset by our disagreement over a few marginal theological issues than he was by the view of a son-in-law who lost no opportunity to make it clear that he regarded Christianity itself as absurd.

"I don't have to justify my attitude to you," he thundered.

In a flash of insight I recognized at once the significance of this retort. By choosing the word "justify," he was betraying his awareness (at the subconscious level at least) that his attitude *could* not be justified—to me or to anyone.

It remained only to take my leave. Embracing him, and kissing him on the cheek, as I had done all my life, I told him, "I love you so much, Daddy."

"That's not important," he replied impatiently. "That's not what you should think about."

I never saw him again.

18

Beached Whale

I entered the Catholic Church with a cold heart, motivated solely by intellectual conviction. There was none of the feeling of "coming home" reported by other converts. I felt almost ashamed. Dr. Spear, the priest-friend of our family mentioned in the account of my mother's death and of my departure for Kelham, lay dying. I was grateful that he would not know what I had done. Newman writes of experiencing for the first time the blessing of living next to a chapel where the Blessed Sacrament was reserved in the tabernacle—"having Christ in bodily presence in one's house, within one's walls, [which] swallows up all other privileges and destroys, or should destroy, every pain."[30] Thanks to the Catholic revival in Anglicanism, which Newman had helped launch, I had enjoyed this blessing all my life long. I expected to dislike my new spiritual home—an expectation that proved, for some time, to be self-fulfilling.

The spiritual pilgrim without expectations has one great advantage, however, over those whose commitment to the

Church engages their hearts. He can suffer neither disillusion nor disappointment. Almost a half century after making my decision, I can honestly say that all my *surprises* have been happy ones. If I had the decision to make over again, I would decide no differently.

Leaving the Episcopal Church was, beyond question, the most difficult thing I have ever done in my life. Looking back I can also say, however—indeed I must say—that entering the Catholic Church was the best thing I have ever done.

Many of my *experiences*, however, were unhappy. The sacrament of penance, which had been a joy to me for two decades, was on occasion painful. An American Redemptorist said to me in the confessional, "I'll bet you never pray"—and refused me absolution. (At the time I was communicating daily at Mass, meditating, and praying the Breviary.) A Dominican spoke to me in the confessional in language suitable for a serial rapist or abuser of little children. Worst of all was the aspect of Catholic life with which I was already familiar: the liturgical wasteland of silent Latin Masses, hastily and perfunctorily celebrated, punctuated by the rattling of rosary beads and rustling of pages in Latin-English missals as the worshipers struggled to follow the action at the distant altar.

On a visit to Mount Saviour's Priory near Elmira, New York, the Prior and former Maria Laach Benedictine, Dom Damasus Winzen, commiserated with me in the strongest of German accents: "American Catholicism, Father, is so *terribly* bourgeois. Vee are trying to do zumsing abowd it."

I would not have put it that way. But I knew what he meant.

I spent my first six months as a Catholic with my Aunt

Sally and Uncle Arthur in Rochester, New York (my mother's sister, married to my father's brother). Though my father had banished me from his home, he continued to write me. Several times he referred to "the step you have apparently taken"—seemingly unable to accept that my decision was final. Unable also to consider that there might be objective reasons for what I had done, he ascribed it to emotional meltdown—and visited a psychiatrist in Boston to discuss his eldest son's mental collapse. He then wrote inviting me to visit this psychiatrist at his expense.

"If I were you, Jay," my Aunt Sally remarked when I showed her this communication, "I wouldn't go within five hundred miles of that psychiatrist."

I assured her I had no intention of doing so. Whether my father could have had me committed to a mental hospital, I do not know. I did know, however, that I had no interest in finding out. I left the letter unanswered—as well as a second one repeating the invitation in more urgent terms.

To support myself, I got a job in the sporting goods department of a large Rochester department store. Anticipating seminary studies and realizing that my only philosophical background was a two-semester survey course at Harvard, I found a priest at St. Bernard's Seminary in Rochester who was willing to tutor me. He gave me a seminary textbook of neo-scholastic philosophy, written in dog-Latin. I found the contents a crashing bore and the arguments unconvincing. When I told him this, he suggested that I consider a line of work other than priesthood. (In 1960 American seminaries were still so full that students were dismissed for the most trivial reasons: Fr. Gordon

Wadhams had told me some of these horror stories. Today the pendulum has swung to the other extreme.)

I also enrolled in a six-week intensive course in German, a language of which I then knew not a single word, at the University of Rochester. This was to prepare myself for theological study at the Canisianum, an international seminary in Innsbruck. I had become aware of this institution through the autobiography of the American Jesuit John La Farge, *The Manner is Ordinary.* He went to the Canisianum following his graduation from Harvard in 1901. A German priest I had met while staying with the Trappists at Spencer had recommended the Canisianum for my own studies.

Conversations with Fr. Gordon Wadhams about his seminary experience in Baltimore convinced me that a free-spirited nonconformist like myself would never survive in a pre-Vatican II American seminary with its Mickey Mouse rules. To the Canisianum I applied, therefore, and received from the Jesuit Regens (Rector) a German letter which I puzzled out with difficulty, given my still meager knowledge of the language. He told me that I could come, even though I lacked a bishop or religious order to sponsor me. I could find a sponsor later.

Humanly speaking I could never have entered the Catholic Church if all I had known of it was the still strongly Irish-American immigrant Church of my native Northeast. Experience of the Church in Europe had shown me that Catholicism had another face. To Europe I returned, therefore, at the end of August 1960, my spirits rising with every mile the ship carrying me eastward placed between North America and me. Save for two brief visits to the United States in 1964 and 1968, I would remain in Europe for almost a decade.

For this lengthy exile I had personal as well as religious reasons. My father's attempts to control my life continued even after I had ignored his request to visit his psychiatrist in Boston. Shortly before my planned departure for Europe my father wrote instructing me to cancel a planned meeting in Holland with my younger brother Dudley and his wife, Rosamond, who were traveling with our fifteen-year-old half-sister Linden. My "emotional state," my father informed me, made such a meeting inadvisable. Clearly the time had come for me to distance myself from him.

* * *

The Canisianum, which I entered in September 1960, was the residence of almost two hundred seminarians from some twenty different countries. Like similar institutions throughout the German-speaking world, and in Rome, it had no faculty of its own. For our studies we attended lectures in town, at the Catholic theological faculty of the state-sponsored University of Innsbruck.

There were a number of Jesuits in the house, in addition to the Regens. One was the celebrated liturgical scholar Joseph Jungmann. His private celebration of a silent Latin "Winkelmesse" ("Mass in a corner," a favorite target of Martin Luther's polemic) gave no hint of the liturgical riches manifest in his writings. Another was Hugo Rahner, elder brother of the more celebrated Karl. Hugo was a historian of the ancient Church, an elegant stylist and speaker whose reputed ambition was to translate his brother's convoluted, interminable German sentences into understandable prose. Pater Hugo (religious order priests are called "Pater," meaning "Father," in German-speaking countries; diocesan priests are called "Herr," meaning "Mister") soon became my confessor. As learned as he was holy, Hugo Rahner was a gentleman to his fingertips, an old-style Jesuit of a kind increasingly rare.

Also in the Canisianum were more than twenty Americans, rejoicing in freedoms undreamed of by their peers back home.[31] Even the seminarians in Rome's North American College were required to spend much of the long summer vacation at a holiday villa. Their contemporaries at the Canisianum, by contrast, roamed Europe on motor scooters and trains like university students the world over.

I found the Americans at the "Can," as we Americans called it, friendly and welcoming. Few ever mastered German. Most were content simply to pick up the rudiments of the language. Typical of this casual attitude was the response of a stalwart Midwesterner to an inquiry about how he was getting on after six months in Innsbruck.

"Aw, it's great," he replied. "Every day you learn more of the language and can say 'Hi' to the fellas."

Like so many others of that era, he left the priesthood a few years after ordination to marry and become "a real father."

From the start I wanted to master German. Building on the foundation of my basic course in Rochester, I spent most of my time on vocabulary and grammar. I still have the slim volume containing Romano Guardini's German translation of the psalms with my penciled translations of unfamiliar words. I chose the Psalter because of my familiarity with the psalms in English. This was a mistake. The psalms have many unusual words. I would have done better to take Mark's Gospel.

The lectures at the university introduced me to a new

world. Karl Rahner's enormous sentences, with numerous asides, parentheses, and examples, were mostly beyond me. It was reassuring to find that many of the German students also found him difficult. One of them, a Bavarian aristocrat and a gifted mimic (his imitations of the German Chancellor Konrad Adenauer addressing the Bundestag were priceless) spent most of one lecture making a grammatical diagram of a single Rahner sentence. It covered two pages.

Unlike the typical German professor, who stands at the podium and reads his lecture (a style Rahner would adopt a few years later first in Munich and then in Münster), Rahner in his Innsbruck years would pace up and down the stage like a caged lion, pausing only occasionally to glance at his notes on the podium. He lectured two semesters on the sacrament of penance, impressing on us the enormous changes this sacrament had undergone in almost twenty centuries.

Each lecture would begin with a statement of the Latin "thesis" that was its subject. A typical example: "We were talking last hour about the twenty-sixth thesis, *Nihil poena sine culpa*" ("no punishment without guilt"). Rahner would spend the rest of the hour developing the implications and consequences of this proposition.

Rahner's dense philosophical and speculative style was relieved by flashes of irony and dry humor, eagerly awaited by his students. These came most often in the homely examples with which he illustrated his points.

Criticizing the idea that grace was a kind of spiritual energy, like electricity, which could be measured (rather than the gift of God's love, which cannot be quantified), Rahner spoke, as he did from time to time, of his elderly mother (a great favorite with the students).

"When my mother..." [loud knocking of knuckles on desks, the accepted form of applause in German universities]. "She is a very pious woman!" [Rahner frowning now and glaring at us through thick glasses, applause louder then ever]. "When my mother goes into a church and finds more than one Mass being celebrated, she is very happy." [Laughter from the students, who understand the reason at once: more Masses means more grace.] "And if you look it up in Pater Noldin [the nineteenth-century Innsbruck Jesuit whose Latin manual of moral theology taught the quantification of grace that Rahner was criticizing], "you will find that my mother is right to be happy. Whether, on the other hand, Pater Noldin is right—that, gentlemen, is another question." [Stamping of feet—the ultimate accolade—and general pandemonium in the lecture hall.]

An example of Rahner's irony that held special significance for me was his comment on an obscure theological dispute in the middle ages. The question had never arisen in antiquity, Rahner said. If it had, however, and if the pope had spoken on the matter *ex cathedra*, "Of course he would have been right—or at least not wrong." Instantly recalling my months' long struggle with this very question only a year before, I was gratified to find the understanding of papal infallibility that had motivated my decision confirmed by this world-renowned theologian.

Still in memory is the response of one of Rahner's Jesuit faculty colleagues when I told him of my difficult journey to the Church.

"It was Catholic books that kept me out of the Church," I told him.

"They should," he replied.

* * *

Rahner's Jesuit colleagues ranged from competent to mediocre. Those who had little to say lectured entirely in Latin. One of them even made announcements in that language. Telling us one day that he would post a list with times of oral examinations[32] in his study-bedroom, he made an exception for the lone female student: *puella non in cubiculo* ("young lady not in the room"). The hilarity this provoked in that pre-feminist age is easily imagined. The same professor would stop speaking in mid-sentence the instant the bell rang signaling the end of the hour, clearly intending to give us an edifying example of Jesuit obedience.

The moral theologian, Pater Miller, seventy-something with close-cropped hair, was a great favorite with the students. His pedagogical method consisted of reading a short passage from the aforementioned Latin manual of Pater Noldin, and then commenting on it briefly before repeating the process with another passage. *This is university teaching?* I asked myself. Harvard, at any rate (the only university then known to me), it clearly was not.

Pater Miller had a special one-semester course, for senior seminarians only (no women allowed) on the sixth commandment: "You shall not commit adultery."[33] This discussed, in rich detail, the sins delicately referred to as "abuses of matrimony." Aware that his students no longer regarded such matters with the gravity that had prevailed in his own seminary days, Pater

Miller told us at the beginning of the course that a former student, one year ordained, had recently returned to tell him, "In just one year in the parish everything you told us about has come up in the confessional."

This too provoked hilarity and comments afterward that the priest must have spent most of his time in the confessional, or that his parishioners must have been unusually inventive—or both.

The Jesuit professor of canon law spoke with a charming Viennese accent comparable (in English) to that of a cultured Irishman or Scot.

"We come now," he announced in his lecture one day, "to one of my hobby horses. This horse has his stall in this beautiful canon 1067, section 2."

I can no longer recall the actual number of the canon or its provisions. It is a safe bet, however, that it had to do with marriage, for the course dealt with little else. A frequently recurring question was what we could do for various classes of people who were invalidly married, had fallen from a Tyrolean alp, and were in danger of death. Since the people in these hypothetical examples were about to pass to a higher tribunal, I could never quite grasp the importance of knowing how to guide them, in their final moments on earth, through the intricacies of canon law. Presumably it had to do with ensuring them Catholic burial, the rules for which were then more stringent than they are today.

* * *

Thursdays in Innsbruck, as in the ecclesiastical universities in Rome, were *vorlesungsfrei* (free of lectures) for students in the theological faculty. (We paid for this with classes on Saturdays.) This was a great boon, since it permitted excursions to the nearby villages and mountains on a weekday when there were few other holiday-makers. In the winter months the skiers among us had the lifts and slopes largely to ourselves.

During the 1960 Christmas holidays I learned to ski by enrolling in a university-subsidized course for students in the village of Ober-Gurgl, at the end of a valley west of Innsbruck. A week's room and board, with daily ski instruction, cost the equivalent of twenty-five dollars. At the end of the week I could come down a slope and make the basic maneuvers without falling down. I never really mastered the art. My skiing resembled Dr. Samuel Johnson's female preacher.[34] The thrill came from being able to do it at all.

An all-day ski tour I made several times started with an early-morning tram ride through Innsbruck to the Patscherkofel, a 2,247-meter-high mountain south of the town. A cable car took us in ten minutes to the saddle between the mountain's two peaks. From there we had a gentle downhill run, diagonally along the slope, of about twenty minutes. Then came a strenuous climb of perhaps two hours. Depending on snow conditions, we would either walk with our skis on our shoulders, or ski uphill with the help of "skins" fastened to the bottom of the skis, which allow them to slide forward but not back.

At the commodious alpine hut just below the summit, we were rewarded for our exertions with a hearty goulash soup and one of the light red wines from South Tyrol (south of the Brenner Pass, culturally Austrian but governed by Italians: a source of keen resentment to people north of the Brenner).

After lunch we rested in the sun outside, the whole world, it seemed, at our feet.

Then came the goal of the entire expedition, the run to the Inn valley far below: sixteen kilometers (ten miles) downhill. No matter that the lower slopes were often without snow, leaving us to walk the last mile through fields with our skis on our shoulders. We emerged in Solbad Hall, where another tram took us back to Innsbruck. The muscles in our legs ached for days, but we had (literally) a mountaintop experience—something to remember gratefully for life.

* * *

My father continued to write me in Innsbruck. Given his treatment of me since my decision to become a Catholic, I felt able to answer only infrequently. Shortly before Christmas 1960, the porter who guarded the entry to the Canisianum came to my room in excitement to announce, "Herr Hughes, you're going to get a phone call from America!"

Overseas phone calls were then not the commonplace affair they are today. This was a person-to-person call booked through the operator. My heart sank. I was certain that the real purpose of the call was to check up on me.

"We just wanted to wish you a Merry Christmas, Jay," my father said as soon as the call came through, "and see how you are."

"I'm fine," I said. (What else could I say?) I had to greet each member of the family in turn. Nothing of any significance was said on either side. As soon as the call was over there would be, I knew, a family conference presided over by my father to discuss the question: "How did Jay sound?" I recognized the good intention behind the call but was troubled by this fresh attempt to interfere with my life based on the assumption that I was an emotional wreck rather than a responsible adult.

The truth was that I was emotionally *spent*. The year-long struggle for theological clarity, overshadowed by knowledge of the pain I must inflict on my father if I could not decide as he wished—followed by the trauma of the final break—had drained my last reserves, leaving me incapable for a time of further moral effort. Reception of the sacraments and personal prayer continued. I even took up yoga, using the book *Christian Yoga* by the French Benedictine J.-M. Déchanet. But I was running on automatic pilot.

At the time I used a different image. More than once during those months, I said to myself, *I'm like a beached whale.*

This would have disastrous consequences before my second year in Innsbruck was over.

19

Shipwreck

The highlight of the summer semester 1961, for me, was a performance of the one-act Gilbert and Sullivan operetta, *Trial by Jury*, with an all-male cast of Canisianum students. The female parts were sung in the normal male range, an octave lower than written. The bride was a Bavarian Benedictine, her unfaithful suitor a Spaniard who spoke no English. I produced, directed, and sang the role of the Judge. A program note gave a synopsis of the plot in German. Despite a few less-than-perfect musical moments, the show was a resounding success, enjoyed by cast and audience alike.

When the semester ended in mid-July, I traveled with two other Americans at the Canisianum to the north German town of Lüneburg, south of Hamburg, for language study at the local Goethe Institute. My relative fluency in German gained me admission to the fourth and highest level of instruction. The classes were entirely in German. We studied idioms, advanced grammar, wrote short essays, and did "re-tellings." These consisted of listening twice over to a brief story in German, 200 words in length, and then reproducing the story ourselves in writing in German. This exercise, common in Germany but apparently unknown in the United States, tests both oral comprehension and written proficiency in the other language.

I worked diligently at this regimen and made rapid progress. By the end of the course I was able to speak and write German with near perfection. Counting the time spent in private study in Innsbruck, I devoted certainly no less than a thousand hours to learning the language. This is the reason, I am confident, why German remains with me today even after long periods of disuse. I can read, speak, and write the language almost as easily as English. Because German is much easier for English speakers to pronounce than, say, French—and because the Lord has given me a good musical ear—Germans often take me for a Dutchman, never for an American or Englishman. Some are kind enough to tell me that I speak their language without an accent.

Lüneburg proved an ideal place for language study. The people in that part of Germany speak an especially pure German and no dialect. I was astonished to find that I could understand customers in the shops and children at play. In Innsbruck we foreigners never understood any of these people. They spoke in dialect.

German dialects are far more distant from standard German (*Hochdeutsch*, originally the language into which Luther translated the Bible) than our local accents are from standard English. In the United States the closest equivalent to dialect is black English ("Ebonics"). Even this comparison fails, however, since black English is the sole language of most of those who speak it. Millions of German speakers, by contrast, speak their native tongue in two different ways. Among each other they speak dialect. With outsiders they speak standard German with the local accent.

In German-speaking lands, speech is not the indicator of social class as it still is in parts of the Anglo-Saxon world, notably in Britain. A Bavarian duke or university professor speaks at home the same dialect used by the local farmers or manual laborers among whom he lives. His standard German may be more grammatical than theirs (because of his higher education level), but his accent is identical.

* * *

I returned to Innsbruck in September 1961 with renewed confidence due to my mastery of German. I still lacked a bishop to sponsor and ordain me. Since arriving at the Canisianum in September 1960, however, the small community of Oratorians at St. Laurentius Parish in Munich had become my home away from home. I was hoping to join the community myself.

In late November 1961 I visited the Regens to tell him of my plans and enlist his support. I had no sooner stated my business than he responded in grim tones:

"Something else has happened."

"What is that?" I asked.

"Another seminarian has brought charges against you."

"What charges?"

"That you have a tendency to homosexuality."

I was devastated. Though completely unprepared for this terrible blow, I knew at once what had happened.

Upon completion of the language course in Lüneburg the

previous August, I had driven, with another American seminarian enrolled with me in the Goethe Institute, south through Germany and France to Lourdes. Hiking one day in the French Alps near Chambéry, we stopped at midday to eat our sandwiches and drink the bottle of wine we had brought with us. Lying side by side in the warm sun, I reached under his shirt, rubbed his back, and attempted to go farther. There was no sexual activity. But I had crossed a boundary. It is always sinful to use another's body for personal gratification. This transgression disqualified me from priesthood forever, the Regens told me.

"Don't take another step!" he said fiercely. "Go sell automobiles, or do anything you like. But don't take another step toward the altar." To avoid an open scandal I could stay at the Canisianum until Christmas. But I could not return thereafter.

Save for this one concession, his treatment of me can only be described as brutal. (Another American at the Canisianum told me decades later that he still bore the psychological scars of his own confrontation with this man over a different matter.) In fairness one must consider, however, that the Regens belonged to the generation that had experienced the Nazi "morality trials," in which scores of Catholic clergy and brothers were accused of homosexual activity, some on the basis of nothing more than an arm on a boy's shoulder or a pat on the back. Who can fault him for thinking he must do all in his power to prevent the recurrence of such a nightmare?

The weeks following this terrible blow were the worst of my entire adult life. I remember walking the streets of Innsbruck and thinking of Abraham preparing to kill his only son. To learn that I could never again stand at the altar as a priest was, after my mother's death, the most bitter blow I have ever received. I was able to confide in two friends only. They told me later that my profound depression had made them fear for my life.

The crisis was made all the more bitter by the knowledge that I had brought it on myself. But why? The seminarian who had denounced me was not a close friend. There was no emotional bond, not even a physical attraction. My behavior had been an act of self-destruction pure and simple. It was like the compulsive act of an alcoholic who, after years of binge drinking and lengthy treatment for alcoholism, has finally landed a good job with the help of generous friends. Seeking a shot of false courage on his first day in his new position, he stops at a bar on the way to work and wakes up weeks later in a distant city. (As an invited guest at Alcoholics Anonymous meetings in my parish hall in Bisbee, I had heard many such stories.)

I must leave it to those with greater knowledge of psychology than mine to discern the reasons for my compulsive behavior. For myself, I believe it had at least an element of the demonic. A Benedictine abbot, talking to me recently about one of his young monks who had abandoned his vows and priesthood less than a year after ordination, said: "That is the hardest thing for me as abbot: when one of our monks in solemn vows leaves. It's the devil trying to get at us."

With no desire to evade responsibility for my behavior—for our Christian faith tells us that Satan can have no power over us without our consent—I believe that this shipwreck (for such it was) was a manifestation of Satan's rage that one of God's sons should wish to serve him as a priest.

* * *

I agonized long over what, if anything, to tell my father. Shortly before leaving Innsbruck at Christmas, I wrote him a brief account of what had happened, appealing to the generous understanding he had so often shown in the past. His response, though brief, contained no reproach. I was especially grateful that he did not say, "I told you so."

He informed family and friends, however, that I would soon be home, with my tail between my legs. With the knowledge that I possess now, I realize that the incident must have amply confirmed his belief that I had never wanted to be a priest and had now found a way to get out of it.

If so, he was mistaken.

20

A Farewell

Dismissal from the Canisianum meant the end of any hope of entering the Munich Oratory. Advisers there (and elsewhere in the years following) urged me to abandon any hope of priesthood in favor of a lay vocation. This counsel, entirely reasonable in the circumstances, I was never able to accept. I believed myself to be a priest already. I had entrusted my priesthood to Our Lady. I believed she was keeping it safe for me and would give it back to me when the time was right.

Following my departure from Innsbruck, the German priest who had recommended the Canisianum to me when we met at St. Joseph's Abbey in Spencer, Massachusetts, in Lent 1960 came generously to my assistance. Through his good offices I obtained a position as *Präfekt*, a combination of teacher and housemaster, at Collegium Augustinianum, Gaesdonck bei Goch. I took up my new duties there at the beginning of February 1962.

"The Gaesdonck" is a Catholic *Gymnasium* or "higher

school" on the site of a fifteenth-century Augustinian canonry (hence the name) established during the *Devotio moderna* movement of the fourteenth and fifteenth centuries that produced the spiritual classic *The Imitation of Christ.* It is situated on the Dutch frontier, some thirty kilometers south of Nijmegen. During the three years I was there, the school enrolled slightly more than four hundred boys, all but a few of them boarders in the *Internat.* I quickly discovered that it was quite different from the boarding school I had experienced in my youth.

The differences started with a clear distinction between academics and everything else. Classroom instruction alone was *Bildung* (education in the strictly academic sense). Everything outside the classroom was *Erziehung* ("upbringing" or "character formation"). *Bildung* was the concern of the faculty, headed by a lay director. A number of them told me they would never send their own children to a boarding school. The proper place for young people, they said, was in the home, not in an *Internat.* This philosophical rejection of an important aspect of the institution by senior staff struck me as curious, to say the least.

The *Internat,* which embraced everything outside the classroom, was headed by a *Präses,* a priest of the large diocese of Münster,[35] which operated the institution. The school proper (but not the *Internat*) received subsidies from the state Ministry of Education in Düsseldorf, which dictated academic requirements in minute detail, including the calendar, course requirements, and even the number and time of examinations. Gaesdonck introduced me to the formidable apparatus of German bureaucracy: ponderous, efficient, and (to a free spirit like myself) stifling.

Boys normally came to Gaesdonck at age ten, living for two

years in a Junior House supervised by matrons. Thereafter they were entrusted to the care of male prefects, normally priests, though this was not a prerequisite. The prefects had auxiliary teaching duties: in my case religion and English language instruction.

Soon after my arrival I was given charge of some seventy boys in four classes, aged roughly thirteen to eighteen. I found that I was sufficiently fluent in German to answer the boys' questions (until the novelty wore off, they were very curious about life in the United States) and express myself clearly. More difficult was sorting out the boys' explanations of their disagreements and quarrels. Cutting through the fog of conflicting claims taxed my powers to the limit. The boys quickly discovered this weakness and exploited it.

I soon discovered that the high school teacher of religion faces unique difficulties. Other subjects in the curriculum require mastery of a body of knowledge. The teacher of religion is imparting not only knowledge, but also values, which have a price tag. Adolescents are beginning, for the first time in their lives, to question the values taught them in childhood. Rebellion is natural. My three years as a religion teacher gave me permanent respect for those who teach this most difficult of all subjects in the high school curriculum.

Teaching English as a foreign language had difficulties of its own. One learns one's native language in childhood, simply by hearing it. Acquiring a foreign tongue—by study, rules, and drill—requires skills and conscious reflection not used in learning one's own language. Teaching English to German boys was a challenge, but fun. I soon realized, however, that it would be easier for me to teach German to English speakers. I could better understand and empathize with their difficulties, having experienced them myself.

My most enjoyable classroom experience at Gaesdonck was an English seminar for college-age boys in the top two classes. They were sufficiently fluent in the language to permit me to hold the entire class in English. We read and discussed the exploits of Sherlock Holmes, short stories by Somerset Maugham, Hemingway's *Old Man and the Sea*, and Lincoln's Gettysburg Address. For a time the seminar included a twelve-year-old American boy who had just entered the school and was learning German. He quickly became a favorite of the older boys. The interplay between them and this still naïve pre-adolescent was highly amusing.

* * *

"There is a call for you from the United States," the German operator said when I answered the phone one afternoon in my apartment at Gaesdonck. I knew at once what it was. My father was dead. It was four o'clock in the afternoon in Germany, ten in the morning on the American east coast. The date was Tuesday, January 14, 1964.

The call was from my younger brother, Dudley. "Daddy died," he said when he came on the line. The funeral was to be Friday, three days later.

"We all want you to come, Jay," he told me, adding with characteristic generosity that he would like to pay for my trip.

I told him I would think about it and cable my decision as soon as possible. Then I went to the chapel, where I could be alone with the Lord in the tabernacle. I prayed for my dear father, using the prayer he had taught me when my mother died. Beyond that, I found that prayer was impossible. I just wanted to sit there and think. There was much to ponder.

* * *

It was two years since I had come to Gaesdonck. Some six months into my first year I had received a letter from my father telling me that he had sold the modest sailing yacht on which he had spent many weeks each summer, adding in the terse epistolary style that characterized every communication I ever had from him since I first went away to boarding school at age twelve, "I have decided I have spent enough money on boats and intend to travel."

He had booked passage for himself and Bina on a transatlantic freighter. There followed a long list of those whom he proposed to visit: just about everyone, it seemed, in the British Isles and continental Europe with whom he had ever had contact since his student days at Oxford in the early twenties. In the middle of this lengthy list was the single pronoun "you." Never has a motive been more transparently clear. The entire purpose of the trip was to see me.

I was neither surprised nor displeased. I had always thought that despite everything, we would meet again. Moreover, time had begun its healing work. I replied saying that I looked forward to showing him the school; that I thought he would be interested in it and like it, though he would probably find our liturgy too "low church" for his taste. In all this I was perfectly sincere.

When the day of his planned departure came, he could not go. I learned this from a letter I received on a day when I imagined him to be already in mid-Atlantic. Written in a changed hand, it told me that on the eve of his departure he had developed a disturbance in his vision and that the doctor had forbidden him to travel. For a time a brain tumor was feared. Some six weeks later he was able to report that there was no tumor, but that the circulation of blood to his head was impaired.

I wrote him my deep sympathy at once, expressing disappointment at not seeing him and Bina and adding that I hoped he would recover sufficiently to make the trip later. It was rescheduled the year following, only to be canceled again when further medical problems arose: a thrombosis or possibly a slight stroke. Characteristically he made light of this. Again I expressed my concern as lovingly as I could by letter, assuring him of my continued prayers.

Shortly before Christmas 1963 he wrote that the doctor had discovered cancer of the rectum. He would have a colostomy immediately after the New Year. I felt in my heart that this was his death sentence, coming as it did on top of all his other ailments. At once I replied as lovingly as possible. He had always prayed, I wrote, in the words of the Litany from the Book of Common Prayer:

> From battle and murder and from sudden death,
>
> *Good Lord, deliver us.*

Now God was answering this prayer by sending him this series of illnesses to invite him to prepare for the great summons home, while leaving him all his faculties so that he could do so properly. I prayed with him, I wrote, that the operation would be successful, and that he would make a full recovery. But whether his death took place soon or not for many years,

I knew he would be ready for it when the call came, fortified with the same triumphant faith that had carried him through so many crises in the past. That faith, I told him, was the most precious thing he had given me. I would be grateful for it always. I assured him of my constant prayers and of my love always.

His reply neither mentioned my letter nor acknowledged its receipt. Instead he wrote about a visit from an older man who had undergone a colostomy ten years previously. He had come, I realized, to give my father courage and hope. How grateful I was to that dear soul. His reward, I reflected, was certain: "I was ill, and you comforted me" (Matthew 25:36). At the same time, it was clear that my father's concentration on his visitor, rather than on what I had written him, said more for his indomitable courage and cheerfulness than for his realism. I could not help but reflect that the visitor almost certainly did not have the further medical problems that had plagued my father for the better part of two years.

Since it was his life that was at stake and not mine, I could permit myself a sober look at the probabilities. Clearly the likelihood of our meeting again in this life was now remote. Despite this, I retained the conviction that he would visit me before the end, if only to say goodbye. Indeed this conviction deepened.

On New Year's Day 1964 my father entered the hospital. I was told later that he felt fine and was in high spirits. In the hospital he spread holiday cheer by stalking about the wards and announcing to his fellow patients and staff, "I'm here for my cancer operation—cancer of the *rectum*!"

That was Daddy, consistent to the end: *semper idem*.

In early January my brother wrote that the operation had been successful. But complications soon arose (I learned later). He had become delirious and could not be kept in bed. Another operation was necessary to repair the damage my father had done to his incision by thrashing about. Then came Dudley's telephone call, telling me it was all over.

* * *

As I sat in the gathering darkness of the chapel, lit only by the flickering light of the tabernacle lamp, I recalled the dream I had not twelve hours before. It was about the sailboat I had bought in Holland two months previously. I was showing the vessel to my father. As always in dreams, things did not correspond to reality. The boat we inspected was very different from the one I had actually acquired. My dream boat was a flat-bottomed craft of typical Dutch design, with leeboards on each side rather than a keel, and leaded window panes in the companionway doors leading to the cabin.

My father was unimpressed and expressed serious doubts about the seaworthiness of this antique craft. His remarks were matter-of-fact and not unfriendly. But he left me in no doubt that I had made an unwise choice.

"Well, I'm sorry you don't like it, Daddy," I told him. "But that's the way the boats are here in Holland."[36]

Recalling the dream in the dim light of the chapel, I realized that my expectation had been fulfilled. My father had come to say goodbye.

I went upstairs to my apartment to send a cable to Bina. How my heart went out to her. How grateful I was to her. I was not quite thirteen when she came to us and made us a family again. I have written already that she had made my father seem ten years younger.

I picked up the telephone and dictated a telegram, spelling out the English words carefully to the German operator:

> Deepest gratitude your twenty-three years unbroken loyalty devotion to Daddy. He was with me last night.
>
> Jay

* * *

Two days later, in the late afternoon of a fine January day, I found myself flying east from New York's Kennedy airport over Long Island Sound. I remembered a family cruise in those waters in June 1944, when my impatience to enter Harvard must have been a trial to the rest of the family. From the air I could see the whole of the Connecticut shore to port, then Fisher's Island, and Block Island off to starboard as we turned north to fly up Narragansett Bay to Providence. The sun was just setting. There was Newport, with the graceful spire of Trinity Church, where my grandfather had served as Rector for thirty-five years. All at once I saw my whole childhood spread out beneath me like a carpet. I knew every inch of those waters. There I had learned to sail, under my father's tutelage. I thought of him lying dead somewhere below and of those I loved best gathered for his funeral the next day.

* * *

After greeting the crowd of relatives and friends at the house in Newport, I asked Jane and Dudley to come upstairs and fill me in on the details of our father's final illness and death. The drugs given to him for his circulatory problems had interacted badly with the medication administered in connection with the surgery. This was the presumed cause of the delirium that had made the second repair operation necessary. Neither of them had had any idea that he was dying, however, until they went to see Daddy two days before the end.

"Jane and I were shocked at Daddy's appearance," Dudley told me. "We could hardly recognize him. He looked so tiny."

I told them I had experienced something similar in other cases. "The gate through which we must pass at death is narrow," I said. "Maybe Daddy had to get smaller somehow before he could slip through."

"He asked for you, Jay," Dudley told me, explaining that some days before his death Daddy had inquired, "Is Jay coming to see me?" They told him they did not consider his condition serious enough to warrant calling me home from Europe. (This was before the alarming change in his appearance.) I said their decision was clearly reasonable in the circumstances.

Then I told them of how I had always expected him to come to say goodbye before the end and of how this expectation had been fulfilled in the dream I had at the very hour, it seemed, when he was dying.

"Poor Daddy," I said sadly, my voice breaking. "He had so much turmoil in his life. How thankful we must be to know he is at peace at last."

* * *

Downstairs the three of us were soon swallowed up in the general conversation and laughter.

"It's like an Irish wake," my Aunt Sally said to me in faintly shocked tones when we found ourselves alone together for a moment in a corner.

"Yes," I replied. "I must say I didn't expect it to be quite like this."

And then, remembering the infectious, high-pitched, shrieking laugh that used to shake my father's whole body and set everyone within earshot laughing with him, I added, "But it's just what he would have wanted."

* * *

We gave him a terrific sendoff the next day at St. Columba's, the little stone church in Middletown of which my father had been rector until his retirement only weeks before. My brother, Dudley, played the organ, and we fairly raised the roof of the small building as we sang some of the stirring old hymns my father loved and had himself sung so often.

The Bishop of Rhode Island pronounced the absolution over the bier at the end of the Mass. As the procession formed, Dudley struck up on the organ the familiar strains of the great Easter hymn: "The strife is o'er, the battle done . . ." With Bina on my arm I followed the coffin down the nave of the church between the densely packed rows of people who had come to pay my father their last tribute and pray for the repose of his soul. How glad I was that on this occasion at least there was no lump in my throat, and that I could sing that grand hymn with the full baritone voice that came to me with my father's genes. The hymn was singularly appropriate, given the strife with which my father's life had been filled.

After the coffin—unvarnished wood with rope handles reminiscent of the sea my father loved so much—had been lowered into the grave in the churchyard outside, the Bishop had the final prayers and committal. I had asked his permission beforehand to have a final prayer. I used the beautiful collect for the Transfiguration in the American Book of Common Prayer, adapting it for the occasion:

> O God, on the mount you revealed to chosen witnesses your only-begotten Son wonderfully transfigured, in raiment white and glistening. Mercifully grant to your servant Dudley, whom you called to the priesthood of your church, that he, being delivered from the disquietude of this world, may be permitted to behold the King in his beauty; where he lives and reigns with you and the Holy Spirit, one God, forever and ever. Amen.

Back at the house in Newport an hour later, I found myself once again in conversation with my Aunt Sally.

"Well, a light has certainly gone out for me," she said.

That was beautiful. But she was mistaken. The light that burned so brightly in my father had not gone out. It had been handed on. It was up to us who loved and survived him to keep it burning brightly.

21

Doctor of Theology

My three years at Gaesdonck coincided with the first three sessions of the Second Vatican Council, which opened on October 11, 1962. With colleagues at the school I followed events at Rome through press reports and the eagerly awaited weekly radio broadcasts of the Swiss Jesuit Mario von Galli.

The Council's first action was to reject the curial candidates for the commissions that would review the draft documents prepared (as the French Dominican Yves Congar complained) for the world of Vatican I. This was a clear signal, even to people distant from Rome, that the "prophets of doom" whom Pope John had criticized in his opening speech were no longer in charge. The "church which never changes"—triumphalistic, complacent, barred, and shuttered against the modern world and all other versions of Christianity save Roman Catholicism—was changing. The Council was replacing it with a more open view of Catholicism: less confident that it had the answer to every difficulty curiosity could propose, more modest in its claims, ready to recognize the existence of truth and sanctity outside the boundaries of the one true Church. This was the model of the Church that had motivated my decision in 1960. At that time it could claim the allegiance of a minority only—a suspect minority. To witness the Council setting the stamp of authenticity on this model was more than I had dared hope for. I felt like a man who backed a dark horse and saw him come home a winner.

A visit to the mammoth Frankfurt Book Fair brought contact with the Herder Verlag, Germany's largest Catholic publisher. This led to translation work and in time to an invitation to join the firm as a full-time employee. The proposed salary was several times the modest stipend I was receiving at the school. The work promised to be interesting: helping develop an English-language version of the theological monthly *Herder Korrespondenz.* But I declined the offer with thanks (though without hesitation), explaining that it would delay achievement of the goal I had never abandoned: priestly ministry in the Catholic Church. For this I prayed daily throughout my time at Gaesdonck, always in the same words: "Not what I want, Lord, but what you want."

Urged by advisers, I began to consider pursuing a doctorate in theology. Inquiries at the faculty of Catholic theology at the University of Nijmegen, a half-hour's drive from Gaesdonck, led to a meeting with the Dutch Dominican, Edward Schillebeeckx. He was encouraging, but I decided that Nijmegen was not the place for me; fortunately, for I lacked the philosophical foundation for study with a speculative theologian like Schillebeeckx.

Christmas 1964 brought an invitation from the bishop of Münster, Josef Höffner, to pursue university studies there in preparation for service as a priest of his diocese. I left Gaesdonck for Münster at Easter 1965. There I once again encountered Karl Rahner, and other luminaries as well: Johann Baptist Metz, Walter Kasper, and Joseph Ratzinger.

Metz, a disciple of Rahner, I found even less intelligible than his master. I understood all his words (I was by now fluent in German), but seldom his meaning. Kasper arrived in Münster when I did, looking at age thirty-two like a novice seminarian. The Dean of the faculty, introducing Kasper at his inaugural lecture, raised a laugh by remarking, "With the inauguration of Herr Professor Kasper, the faculty of Catholic theology in the University of Münster experiences a palpable rejuvenation."

Kasper provoked mirth himself in a later lecture. Searching for an example of the theological concept "grace," Kasper said, "When you are sitting in the confessional, and someone comes whose last confession was more years ago than you are old, *that* is grace." He went on to a professorship in Tübingen and thence to be bishop of the diocese in which that university is located, Rottenburg-Stuttgart, and finally a curial cardinal.

Joseph Ratzinger's lectures on the Church in the summer semester 1965 were the most beautiful I have ever heard at any of the three universities I have attended, on any subject. After every lecture, one wanted to go into a church and pray. Ratzinger's flowing sentences and paragraphs, enriched by frequent citations from Scripture and the Church Fathers (especially Augustine, the subject of his doctoral dissertation) were so polished that he was said to speak *druckreif*—"print ripe."

The spoken lecture could have been transcribed and printed without alteration.

Ratzinger could often be seen riding around Münster on a bicycle, wearing a beret. He lectured three times weekly at 8:15 in the morning. Evidence of his popularity was the presence among his hearers of a number of people from the town, who came to hear him before going to their offices. Present too was a Protestant student from South Africa whose imminent conversion was confidently predicted by the Catholic students: "Ratzinger overwhelms even the strongest man."[37] This jest would prove prescient. Two decades later the German journalist Peter Seewald would abandon his communist atheism and return to the Catholicism of his childhood as the result of his conversations with Cardinal Ratzinger (as he then was), recorded in the books *Salt of the Earth* and *God and the World.*

Anticipating university teaching in the United States, I looked for a dissertation topic with relevance in my own country. I got no further than "something in the area of church-state relations," when I was urged by Abbot Laurentius Klein of the Benedictine Abbey of St. Matthias in Trier to investigate the question of Anglican orders, declared by Pope Leo XIII in 1896 to be "absolutely null and utterly void."

Klein had established an institute for Anglican studies in Trier, and in preparation had sent two of his young monks to study theology in Oxford. I told Klein that the horse he was urging me to mount had been flogged dead. He was confident that, if I studied the subject in depth, I would find fresh material. Though skeptical, I allowed myself to be persuaded.

With the benefit of hindsight, I believe that my original idea was better. A dissertation on some aspect of the church-state relationship would have taken me into an area that remains relevant and important today. The question of Anglican orders brought me temporary notoriety. But it proved something of a cul-de-sac, even before the disintegration of Anglicanism we are witnessing today (in the United States especially) rendered the question moot.

Shortly after arriving in Münster, I asked Joseph Ratzinger to accept me as a doctoral candidate, with the topic of Anglican orders for my dissertation. His response was friendly but regretful. He already had more doctoral candidates than he could handle and could not accept another. Following my rejection by Ratzinger, I applied to his faculty colleague Erwin Iserloh. A priest of the Münster diocese, Iserloh had done his own doctoral studies under Joseph Lortz, the first German Catholic historian to take a sympathetic view of Martin Luther. Known as conservative in theology and a hard taskmaster, Iserloh gave me minimal guidance and then subjected my work to withering criticism. This made him an excellent director for a topic that was bound to be controversial.

* * *

My research on Anglican orders took me for months on end to England. I enjoyed the hospitality of the Benedictines at St. Benet's Hall in Oxford, while I worked in the Bodleian Library, and at Downside Abbey, where I studied the papers of two central figures in the Roman investigation of Anglican orders in 1896: the Downside monk (and later cardinal) Aidan Gasquet and his more learned lay friend Edmund Bishop—the source of most of what was reliable in Gasquet's writings. I also studied in the library at Kelham, renewing friendships there while staying with the Catholic Holy Ghost Fathers a few miles distant. At York I studied the papers of Lord Halifax, a central Anglican figure in 1896. And in London I searched the archives at Archbishop's House, Westminster.

Comparing the manuscript of Gasquet's diary in the mid 1890s with the version he published later, I discovered significant alterations. In March 1895, for instance, Gasquet reported that Pope Leo XIII had told Cardinal Vaughan of Westminster that he (the pope) had the opinions of the best authorities on Anglican orders, and that it was clear they were invalid.

Had Gasquet published this, Anglicans would have seized upon the statement as proof that, a full year before the formal investigation of the orders, the pope had already decided the question, and that no serious study was ever intended. Gasquet's solution for this difficulty was simple: he altered the pope's words. The version published in 1911 as *Leaves from My Diary* had Leo saying:

> He had had the opinions of men qualified to judge; from these, he added, it was clear that *without a full examination*, no change in the present attitude of the church would be possible. [Emphasis supplied.]

More significant was my discovery in the Westminster archives of a 1910 letter disclosing that only four of the eight members of the papal commission appointed to study the question had pronounced Anglican orders invalid.[38] Abbot Klein's prediction that I would discover fresh material was proving correct.

* * *

My research focused principally on the writings of the English Jesuit, Francis Clark. He had defended Leo XIII's 1896 condemnation of Anglican orders in two books: *Anglican Orders and Defect of Intention* (1956) and *Eucharistic Sacrifice and the Reformation* (1960). At a first reading, the apologetic fortress that Clark had constructed appeared impregnable.

After long and weary toil, however, I achieved a breakthrough. I found that the quotations from Catholic theologians that Clark had used to support his argument about defective intention in Anglican ordinations were truncated. In case after case Clark omitted material that contradicted what he was trying to prove. In late 1966 I published my findings, comparing Clark's quotations with the unabridged originals.[39]

Though Clark never responded to the article, it had an interesting sequel. During a brief visit to Rome in October 1967, I called on Father Clark, who was then teaching at the Gregorian University. I encountered a man distraught. As soon as he learned that I was the author of the offending article, he became menacing. My article had led people in England, he told me, to believe that the question of Anglican orders, previously regarded as settled, was now open. This would have the most serious consequences, he warned, seeming to imply that I could be the first victim. I emerged from the interview shaken, fearful that Clark might try to prevent my return to priestly ministry in the Catholic Church.

* * *

Leo XIII had condemned Anglican orders in 1896 not merely because of an alleged defect of intention, however. More important was the alleged defect of form. *Apostolicae curae*, the papal document that condemned the orders, argued that the English Reformers had rejected the doctrine of Eucharistic sacrifice.

They framed their new ordination rites to express this rejection. Hence these new forms could not convey priesthood in the Catholic sense, defined as "sacrificing priesthood," as distinct from priesthood as understood by the Reformers: a mere ministry of word and sacrament.

Anglican apologists had responded that what the Reformers rejected was not the Church's authentic teaching, but rather "late medieval errors" about Eucharistic sacrifice. Not so, Clark argued. In his second book, *Eucharistic Sacrifice and the Reformation*, Clark showed there was little evidence of such errors. He cited text after text from late medieval theologians to show that Catholic teaching about Eucharistic sacrifice in the early sixteenth century was entirely orthodox. The Reformers were familiar with this teaching, Clark argued, and it was this they rejected.

Clark's work was impressive. The more I studied it, however, the clearer it became that it suffered from a fatal weakness. Clark offered no explanation for the dynamic power and popular success of the Reformers' new theology (certainly in Germany, less in England), save as the victory of error over truth.

To my shame I must confess that I had never really understood the Reformation. As an Anglo-Catholic, I had regarded Protestantism as the enemy within the gate. The Reformation, which gave birth to this foe, should never have happened, in my view. I had no desire to come to grips with a movement I considered utterly mistaken.

My research on Anglican orders forced me, for the first time, really to study Luther and the other Reformers. I discovered the positive concern behind their negative polemic: the wish to defend the "pure gospel"—the good news that we are brought into a right relationship with God ("justified" in technical language) not on the basis of our goodness, but of his. We are saved, in other words, by grace, not by our "good works." The latter are our *grateful response* to God's gift of salvation, not the prerequisite for receiving it. This is the doctrine that produced the joint Catholic-Lutheran declaration on justification signed in Augsburg on October 31, 1999.

In attacking Eucharistic sacrifice, the Reformers were polemicizing not against some "pure" theology of the Mass developed by academic theologians in their studies—the source of all the texts cited by Clark. The Reformers were concerned, rather, with the vast number of Masses being celebrated every day—far in excess, I learned, of any conceivable pastoral need. The real object of the Reformers' attacks was the often tortured defense of this practical Mass system offered by medieval preachers and theologians.

Especially questionable was the theology of Mass "fruits" distributed in accordance with the celebrating priest's intention. In the sixteenth century it was common teaching that since the fruits of each Mass were limited, it was better to belong to a parish of a hundred souls than to one of a thousand, since those in the smaller parish received a larger share of the Mass fruits when the priest offered Mass for his flock.

While not formally heretical, the quantification of grace this teaching embodied—and even more the suggestion that it was possible by a multiplication of Masses and other religious practices to earn salvation for one's self and others—is difficult to reconcile with the central Gospel truth that we are saved by God's grace, not by our good works. My research uncovered numerous examples of this theology, which Clark had completely overlooked.

This was the focal point of the Reformers' attack. How, they asked, could the teaching that the Mass is a sacrifice be reconciled with the central message of the Letter to the Hebrews: that Jesus had offered "one sacrifice for sins forever," which could never be added to or repeated? Challenged on this point, the Catholic apologists could do little but repeat that the Mass was a sacrifice; that the church had always so taught; and that the denial of this central truth was unheard of.

The reason for this feeble response, I learned, lay in the lack of previous theological reflection on Eucharistic sacrifice. Throughout the later Middle Ages, theologians had concentrated ever more narrowly on transubstantiation and on the philosophical problems of the real presence of Christ's body and blood in the consecrated bread and wine. Clearly the inability of the Catholic apologists in the early Reformation period (during which the English Reformers composed their new ordination rites) to explain how the Mass could be a sacrifice if Jesus' sacrifice was all-sufficient and unique, was crucial in judging their denial of Eucharistic sacrifice.

* * *

Newman called the question of Anglican orders "dreary." Most people will agree. Studying it forced me, however, to study questions of central importance: Eucharistic sacrifice, but also the Church's teaching about its ordained ministry (in technical language, "ministerial priesthood").[40]

Apostolicae curae speaks of "sacrificing priesthood" and contrasts it (as we have seen) with the non-sacrificing ministry of word and sacrament conferred by the new Anglican rites. But was "sacrificing priesthood" an adequate description of the Church's teaching about its ordained ministry? In 1896 Catholics assumed that it was. *Apostolicae curae* did not argue the point, being content to cite language from the Council of Trent.

To Trent I went, therefore, and discovered that the council never intended to state the Church's full doctrine of ministerial priesthood. The first sentence of Trent's dogmatic decrees on the sacrament of orders says that only as much Catholic doctrine was being set forth as was necessary "to refute the errors of our time."[41]

That Christ is a sacrificing priest is the clear teaching of Hebrews. Calling the Church's ordained ministers sacrificing priests, without careful explanation, is another matter. Significantly, the *Catechism of the Catholic Church* avoids the term, preferring to emphasize the uniqueness of Christ's priesthood and sacrifice with a quotation from St. Thomas Aquinas: "Only Christ is the true priest, the others being only his ministers" (No. 1545).

* * *

The results of my doctoral research, summarized above, resulted in two books of some 350 pages each: *Absolutely Null and Utterly Void: The Papal Condemnation of Anglican Orders 1896* (1968), and *Stewards of the Lord: A Reappraisal of Anglican Orders* (1970). The first book did not treat the question of validity directly. It recounted the backstairs maneuvering in England and at Rome which resulted in Leo XIII's declaration that the orders "were and are absolutely null and utterly void."

Stewards of the Lord examined the Reformation controversy over Mass and priesthood. It argued that the Reformers' denial of Eucharistic sacrifice arose from a practical Mass system, and the justification for it given by theologians and preachers, which obscured the uniqueness of Christ's saving work. The book also questioned whether defining the Church's ordained ministry simply as "sacrificing priesthood" adequately reflected the fullness of Catholic doctrine. And it showed that the authorities cited by Francis Clark to support the alleged defect of intention in Anglican orders point in the diametrically opposite direction, if read in context.

Looking back, I believe that *Stewards of the Lord* was too narrowly conceived as a refutation of Clark's two books. Like any refutation, this one may have been faulty. The only critic to have so argued, to my knowledge, was Clark's fellow Jesuit, Maurice Bévenot, who in a brief review called my book "a work of utter destruction."[42]

Clark himself chose to ignore my work, republishing *Eucharistic Sacrifice and the Reformation* in a new edition some years later without acknowledging the existence of a book that refuted its central claims. Not until 1995 did Clark take cognizance of my arguments set forth in my keynote address to the international conference on the centenary of *Apostolicae curae* and published in the London *Tablet*. Even then, however, Clark still declined to engage. His article, courteous in tone, expressed pained surprise that anyone could disagree with him—still oblivious of the existence of a book, published a quarter of a century before, that gave detailed reasons for this disagreement.[43]

* * *

The last word goes to the late George Tavard. A theologian of international repute, Tavard was the severest critic of *Stewards of the Lord* at the time it was published. Two decades later, in a book that contained much fresh material on the question of Anglican orders, Tavard made a gracious retraction:

> I confess that my critique of *Stewards of the Lord* was excessive... The main lines of Hughes's analysis are vindicated by the archival documents that have [since] been published.[44]

22

"We Leave It to God What Has Really Happened."

In the autumn of 1967 Bishop Höffner sent word that he was willing to ordain me the following January. The goal of my eight-year pilgrimage was finally in sight. Still unresolved, and for me crucial, was the question of conditional ordination. Absolute ordination would entail my tacit admission that I had never been a priest. This I could not in conscience accept. Conditional ordination would respect my conscientious conviction, while giving the Catholic Church the assurance it needed that my priesthood was authentic. I had raised the matter several times with Bishop Höffner, always as a question, never as a condition *sine qua non*.

I was still without an answer to this question as I prepared to visit the bishop at ten o'clock in the morning of Friday, January 26, 1968. Before doing so, I stopped in the cathedral for prayer. Emerging through the cloister, I stopped at the fresh grave of a cathedral canon, piled high with flowers. He had been buried the previous day. I had not known the man, but tributes I had read attested that he was a zealous and holy priest. Standing by the grave, I prayed that I might take up the banner that had fallen from his hands.

It was with no little trepidation that I walked the short distance across the cathedral square to the bishop's house and rang the bell, aware that the next half hour would determine the whole course of my future life.

Once again, as in previous conversations, I raised the question of conditional ordination, telling Höffner that the orders of the Episcopalian bishops who had ordained me deacon and priest respectively were not identical with the orders condemned by Pope Leo XIII in 1896: these prelates could trace their consecration, through others, to Old Catholic and other prelates recognized by Rome as true bishops.

Verifying that would require a Roman investigation, the bishop responded, "and that could take years." We were clearly on the brink of the decision I had long sought, and it appeared that it would be negative. Inwardly I steeled myself to tell Höffner that, in these circumstances, I must withdraw.

Before doing so, however, I played my trump card. With little hope that it would have any effect, I drew from my pocket the letter about my case written eight years previously by Père Philippe.[45] As by the touch of a magic wand, the entire atmosphere was transformed. The bishop had no sooner read the document I placed in his hands than he announced, to my astonishment and delight: "It is clear. I must ordain you conditionally."

I walked out of the bishop's house on air, conscious that

the angels had been with me, yet scarcely able to believe that the hopes and prayers of the past eight years were about to be fulfilled.

At seven o'clock the next morning, in the bishop's private chapel and in the presence of seven priest-friends, I received: tonsure, four minor orders, sub-diaconate, and *sub conditione,* diaconate and presbyterate (priesthood). A framed certificate testifying to this hangs beside me as I write these lines. I believe it to be unique in the world.

At the end of this ninety-five minute ceremony, Bishop Höffner said to me: "Herr Hughes, we welcome you into the presbyterate of this diocese. We have given you the orders of deacon and priest conditionally, and we leave it to God what has really happened."

I had never told Höffner about entrusting my priesthood to Our Lady and asking her to give it back to me when the time was right. This gave added significance to his subsequent action. Turning toward Mary's statue in his chapel, Höffner intoned the Marian hymn, *Salve Regina* ("Hail, Holy Queen").

A few hours later I visited the community of Poor Clare nuns in Münster who had befriended me and prayed for me, to tell them how our prayers had been answered that morning. When I related my long-ago prayer to Mary, and the bishop's choice of Mary's hymn, I could see that I was not the only person who was deeply moved.

* * *

Two days later my picture was on the front page of the London *Guardian*, with a full-column account of the quiet, private ceremony in Münster. The information came from Martin

Redfern, head of the publishing house of Sheed & Ward, which had contracted to publish my two books on Anglican orders. Hoping that my conditional ordination might constitute a precedent for others, and fearful that it might later be denied if there was no contemporary report of what had happened, I wanted the event to be a matter of public record. The week before the ceremony, therefore, I had sent a background statement to Redfern, embargoed until he received from me the telegram I dispatched from Münster's main post office immediately after the ordination: "Release. Hughes."

The *Guardian* article unleashed a storm of controversy, as English Catholics, who had long made the invalidity of Anglican orders the cornerstone of their polemic against the Church of England, rushed before television cameras, and into print, to insist that there must have been some mistake: everyone knew that Anglican clergy were Protestant ministers, and their archbishops laymen in fancy dress. Requests for statements, interviews, and a personal appearance in British television came flooding in on me. Upon learning that my acceptance of such invitations could embarrass Bishop Höffner, I declined them all.

On the day following my conditional ordination, I celebrated Mass again for the first time in eight years. One of the two priests who assisted me (he is now a bishop in Germany) said to me in the sacristy afterward, "You were so assured."

"I'm not doing this for the first time," I replied.

23
Münster

Although three of my four and a half years in Münster were a time of waiting, with no assurance that the waiting would be rewarded, these were happy years. Despite the often leaden skies and frequent rain, I grew to love the town, regarding it as one of the most beautiful in West Germany.

The Münsteraner, with the inhabitants of the surrounding province of Westphalia, are overwhelmingly Catholic. Their attachment to the ancient faith found expression in the saying attributed to a typical representative of this deeply reserved, stolid race: "We don't care what they do down there in Rome. We're staying Catholic."

During the Nazi period, Münster was the only city of significant size not visited by Adolf Hitler. He never cared to risk the chilly reception. Bishop of Münster during those years was Clemens August Count von Galen, known as "the Lion of Münster" because of his resistance to Nazi tyranny. This culminated in three sermons he preached in 1941, denouncing euthanasia in German mental hospitals and Hitler's persecution of the church. Copied and distributed secretly throughout wartime Germany, the sermons were also dropped over Germany by Allied warplanes.

A fervent patriot, von Galen opposed Hitler as traitor to the best traditions of his country. Limited in outlook, however, by his nineteenth-century nationalism, von Galen found Germany's defeat bitter. When British troops entered Münster in 1945, he issued a statement deploring "this day of shame, when the enemy enters our city."

In recognition of his courage von Galen received a cardinal's hat from Pope Pius XII in February 1946. A month later death removed him from a world that had changed forever. He was beatified by Pope Benedict XVI in October 2005. His tomb in the Münster cathedral is always decorated with burning candles and fresh flowers.

The same was true, during my Münster years, of a grave in the city's Central Cemetery. It contained the body of Sister Euthymia, member of a nursing order who had died in 1955. Of Westphalian peasant stock and a kind of German counterpart to Ste. Thérèse of Lisieux, she had spent her life working in the hospital laundry and kitchen, largely unnoticed. After her death reports of answered prayers by those who sought her intercession resulted in her beatification by Pope John Paul II in 2001. I often visited Sister Euthymia's grave to invoke her prayers for a return to priestly ministry, and for the success of my doctoral studies. Even on rainy days I was seldom alone. I was happy to include her in the dedication of *Stewards of the Lord*:

For all who have helped, especially

St. Jean-Baptiste-Marie Vianney

Pope John XXIII

Ste. Thérèse de Lisieux

Sr. Maria Euthymia

* * *

At the end of the private ordination ceremony described above, Bishop Höffner announced that he was appointing me Kaplan (Associate Pastor) of the recently founded parish of St. Thomas More in Münster. I had already founded a parish choir there, which I directed myself. I was thus well known to the parishioners and their pastor, like myself a priest of about forty. Simultaneously Höffner freed me from parish duties, so that I could complete the doctorate. The faculty had already accepted my dissertation. The Rigorosum (oral examinations in eight major areas of theology) was still ahead of me. I slogged away at the preparations through most of 1968, taking the first four exams in the spring, the remaining four toward year-end. I received the German "Dr. theol." in February 1969, along with a dozen other candidates. At the celebratory banquet afterward, the other foreigners who received the degree with me asked me to give the speech of thanks, in recognition of my fluency in the language of our hosts.

Shortly thereafter I saw in the London *Tablet* the announcement of a new English-language faculty of theology to be established at the ancient Catholic University of Louvain, recently renamed Leuven when the French-speaking half of the university was forced to relocate because of Belgium's language war. I applied for a position and was appointed visiting professor of Church history and Anglicanism for the autumn semester 1969.

As a result of an American lecture tour in March 1969, I had already received offers of teaching positions at the Jesuit universities in Detroit and St. Louis. With permission from the diocesan authorities in Münster, I accepted the invitation from St. Louis to begin in January 1970 following my teaching in Leuven.

On the last Sunday of September 1969, I took leave of the parishioners at St. Thomas More, conscious that the German chapter of my life was ending. I told them about the farewell of Angelo Roncalli (later Pope John XXIII), after almost a decade as apostolic delegate in Bulgaria. He spoke about the custom of Irish Catholics, who put a lighted candle in their windows at Christmas to tell Mary and Joseph—who had found no room in the inn on the first Christmas—"Someone is waiting for you here." Roncalli said that he was putting a candle in his window to show all Bulgarians, wherever they might be, that a welcome awaited within. I told them,

> After almost a decade in Germany, I should like to say: I too am putting a candle in my window. It burns for Germany, and for all who speak its language—one that I shall always be happy to hear, and happy to speak.
>
> As I was packing my belongings this past week, I found a letter I wrote to Bishop Höffner in January 1968 to thank him for his kindness and tell him of the reception I had received the first time I offered the Holy Sacrifice

> here in our parish. Here is some of what I said: "The respect and love that I experienced overwhelmed me. They were clearly not recognition for anything I had done. They were, rather, the expression of the regard that Catholics have for the priest as representative of Jesus Christ. This deep respect, out of all proportion to our deserving, is humbling. But it also motivates us priests to be truly the men the people take us for and love."

I was especially grateful, I said, to those who had expressed appreciation of my preaching.

> I cannot imagine that I shall ever again have such attentive hearers as I have had here. I certainly do not expect them in the university lecture hall that awaits me. Today, however, I would like to say something you have not heard me say before: You can forget everything, really everything, you ever heard me say from this pulpit—with one exception. Never forget that a priest of Jesus Christ stood before you, and in his somewhat quaint German and accent, but with all the inner conviction and fervor at his command, bore witness that these things are true, now and for all time:

- that this world, with all its suffering and injustice, is still God's world;
- that God governs the course of this world and of each of us in it;
- that he loves each one of us, and you personally, with a love beyond the power of words to describe, a love that will never let us go.

God's love never ceases, never fails, is never distant from us. Even in times of darkness, indeed in the deepest darkness of our self-chosen guilt and sin, God, and God's never-failing love, are close to us. God is patient. God is willing to wait. Weeks? Months? No, far longer. God will wait years, if need be a whole lifetime, for someone to turn, to repent, to say yes to him and to his love.

In this love we part. What awaits us none of us can know. We live in a time of rapid change: in the Church, in society, in our personal lives. For many that is unsettling. One day, however, we shall be able to look back and see what a privilege it was to have lived in such a time. We shall be able to say, "We were there when a new world, and a renewed Church, were struggling to be born."

What is coming, none of us can know. But we do know *who* is coming. And him I joyfully proclaim to you: "Jesus Christ, the same yesterday, today, yes and forever!" (Hebrews 13:8).

24

Reentry

At my return to the United States in January 1970, I had been away for almost a decade. I had left in 1960 to escape pre-Vatican II American Catholicism. I found in the German-speaking world a spiritual home more congenial than any I had dared hope for.

In place of hastily celebrated silent Latin Masses, I found reverent liturgies with genuine popular participation. German-speaking Catholics, I discovered, had been singing hymns at Mass for centuries. Many of the melodies were familiar to me from my Anglican past. In place of the sociologically monolithic immigrant Church still flourishing in 1960 in the American Northeast, I found myself in a larger and more heterogeneous world. German-speaking Catholicism was a cross section of society. The parish clergy, all university educated, were certainly not all intellectuals. But their reading was not confined to the sports pages of the newspaper, and they were not embarrassed to talk about ideas.

I felt spiritually at home in Germany. Like most expatriates, however, I remained aware that I was an alien—thinking, feeling, reacting differently from the people among whom I lived and whose positive traits I greatly admired. It was always a delight, therefore, to encounter other native English-speakers. Even if they were not Americans, we could "let down our hair" together and share amusement and irritation at aspects of German life that, viewed through Anglo-Saxon eyes, looked odd or even preposterous.

Europe's long history, rich in achievement but also in tragedy, is both a blessing and a burden to that history's heirs. It gives them a richness and depth too often lacking in the New World. Europeans appreciate life's complexity and tragedy better than Americans with our cheerful and often superficial optimism. At the same time, Europe's long history also erects barriers, limiting freedom of action and thought in ways Americans would never accept.

A Belgian priest deeply involved in issues of social justice told me during my German years about visiting the headquarters of the United Auto Workers in Detroit. His hosts offered to give him introductions to trade union leaders in Brussels.

"Forget it," he replied. "They're socialists. As a Catholic priest, I can't even get in the front door."

The collapse of communism in 1989 may have dismantled that barrier. But others remain. German friends were incredulous when I told them that one of my close friends in Bisbee had been an atheist lawyer. Such a friendship would be inconceivable in a small town in Germany, they assured me.

When all the negatives that irritate the citizen of the New World living in the Old have been added together, however, they pale beside the positive values. My German years greatly broadened my horizon. They continue to enrich me today: both intellectually and spiritually.

Germany transformed my taste in church art and architecture. Previously I was enamored of the old, embodied in English cathedrals like Canterbury and York Minster. Germany opened my eyes to the new. The best of the strikingly modern churches erected since World War II amid the ruins of German cities convinced me that a church built today should speak to today's world and not mimic the past, however beautiful. Otherwise we risk constructing museums: interesting and beautiful, but with no relevance to modern life. Returning to the United States and having to worship in churches that, all too often, are sadly inferior imitations of the past was a culture shock.

* * *

Save for my brief trip home for my father's funeral in January 1964, I was continuously in Europe from 1960 until the summer of 1968, when I accepted a faculty appointment at a summer institute at Marist College in Poughkeepsie, New York. How things had changed! The liturgy, no longer silent, had become a happy-happy celebration of human togetherness. A clearly remembered homily conveyed nothing beyond the message, "I'm so happy I can be here with all you wonderful, beautiful people." This was worship? I had never experienced anything remotely similar—certainly not in Germany, where the pre-conciliar liturgical and youth movements, and biblical studies, had prepared the ground for many of Vatican II's reforms.

A faculty colleague and fellow priest, and a liberated nun,

spent much of the six weeks behaving like adolescents, unable to control their raging hormones. Had I wanted to try my hand at fiction, I could have written a highly amusing novel about that madcap summer.

My impression of a Church in disarray was deepened by experiences at the American College in Leuven, my residence for the closing months of 1969. I found the seminarians rearranging the liturgy to conform to their notions of propriety. When I questioned this, I was told that all the elements were still there, even if their order had been changed. My contention that the liturgy was something given to us by the Church, not something we made up afresh each time, met with incomprehension. Obviously I was "a conservative" (i.e., unenlightened).

A newly ordained priest in the college, celebrating Mass on All Souls Day, eliminated from the prayers provided by the Church all petitions for the departed, and prayed simply for ourselves: that our faith might be a light to others, etc. What could have been viewed charitably as youthful folly became more troubling when I learned that the man's mother had recently died.

Over time I came to realize that I was experiencing desacralization—a reaction against what those responsible for these abuses considered the excessive other-worldliness of the pre-conciliar Church. The transcendent was out. Liturgy was a gathering of the like-minded for moral uplift, mutual encouragement, and a "meaningful worship experience."

Invited in the early 1970s to celebrate Mass for a community of religious Sisters in St. Louis, I was informed on arrival that we would not be using the chapel. Instead I was expected to offer the Holy Sacrifice seated at a card table in the community's recreation room. The telephone, also in the room, rang and was answered throughout.

The organizers (or were they "facilitators"?) of a "Young Adults Social Action Weekend," which I experienced shortly after coming to St. Louis, also preferred the lounge of their conference center to the well-furnished chapel for Mass. The liturgical texts had been specially composed for the occasion, the opening "collect" running thus:

> Prayer can begin in different ways. It can start the first time we become aware of another's need, the first time someone really touches us. Prayer is reaching out to one another in love.

The offertory and post-communion prayers were in the same vein. None contained a single petition, nor were any of them addressed to God.

The search for readings had clearly taken little time. Paul's hymn to love in 1 Corinthians 13 was an obvious choice, though the nun who read it changed Paul's words to read: "When I became a woman, I put away childish things." (*Would that she had*, I thought.) Not so the "Gospel," which began:

> Seeing the crowds, he went up on the mountain, and when he sat down his disciples came to him. And he opened his mouth and taught them saying: "I have a dream today…"

What followed came not from Scripture but from Martin Luther King Jr.

Liturgical banalities like these (another: the female undergraduate who offered, amid laughter, a petition at a Jesuit-led noonday liturgy in St. Louis "for all those who have had a difficult morning") were the background to the book I wrote during my first months in St. Louis: *Man for Others: Reflections on Christian Priesthood*. Published first in England, then in the United States, and subsequently in German translation, it protested against the liturgical and theological chaos I experienced in American Catholicism in the early post-conciliar period. The expression of my deeply held, indeed passionate, conviction about the need to maintain at whatever cost the tension between the vertical and horizontal elements in faith and worship, the book almost wrote itself.

Amid the "anything goes" atmosphere I encountered upon joining the Divinity School faculty at St. Louis University, it was a delight to discover in the St. Louis Benedictines an intact community that, though then small and struggling, was still in touch with age-old Catholic tradition. I have written already of my gratitude when, three decades later, they made me a Confrater of their community.

25
PROFESSOR

"Jay, you're a born pedagogue."

A colleague said this to me in Newark in 1953, after watching me teach boys to serve at the altar.

Teaching came easily to me. I enjoyed it and was confident that I was a good teacher: not brilliant, but certainly competent.

But university teaching? For a long time I found it difficult to see myself in that role. My image of the profession had been shaped by my teachers at Harvard. I could not see myself in their league. Over time I came to realize that few were. I was encouraged when Josef Schreiner, the popular professor of the Old Testament in Münster, who often celebrated Mass at St. Thomas More and had heard me preach there many times, told me when I was leaving, "You will have great success as a teacher."

My teachers in Innsbruck and Münster belonged to the magisterial tradition still taken for granted in the Old World.

Most of them read their lectures from a manuscript. Students were supposed to hear in class everything they needed to know to pass the examination. Critical discussion of the professor's arguments was confined to student conversations outside the lecture hall.

German students exhibited enormous industry in producing a *scriptum* of the professor's lectures, a verbatim transcript (so far as this was possible) of everything the *great man* had said, compiled from shorthand notes. These *scripta* were duplicated and sold to fellow students at modest cost. I still have the *scripta* of Joseph Ratzinger's lectures. They are excellent .[46]

My teaching in Leuven in the autumn of 1969 followed the pattern with which I was familiar. For every lecture I had a full manuscript. This was not as polished as that which I still take into the pulpit on Sunday. But it was carefully organized, detailed, with special attention to transitions and continuity. An American student (clearly a history buff) told me after class one day, "Gee, Father, I really love that history."

A year later a priest pursuing a doctorate at the St. Louis Divinity School would say the same, in more elevated language.

* * *

St. Louis University is run by the Society of Jesus. I remembered the St. Joseph Abbey Trappist, Fr. Raphael Simon, telling me during my visit there in Lent 1960 that he didn't think the Jesuits were for me: "They can be very arbitrary." A diocesan priest working for any religious order soon learns that he is an outsider. Decisions are made in the community's private quarters and may be communicated to him (if they are communicated at all) through unofficial channels.

This happened to me at the Divinity School of St. Louis University, when students told me following one summer vacation that a survey course I had previously taught, and to which I had been assigned at the end of the previous semester, had been given to a newly hired female colleague. When I confronted my Jesuit department chairman about this, he replied blandly: "Oh, yes, I want her to get the overview." The failure to notify me of this decision was deemed worthy neither of explanation nor apology.

This incident was typical of my experience at the Divinity School, a chapter of my life that resembled nothing so much as a Kafka novel. Illustrating this statement with examples would risk obscuring my high regard for the Society of Jesus at its best. I refer readers who would like to know more, therefore, to the book *King's Pawn*[47] by the St. Louis Jesuit, George Dunne, an account of the author's harassment and mistreatment by colleagues and superiors at St. Louis University. I read Dunne's book with a sense of *déjà vu*, having had remarkably similar experiences at the same institution myself, a quarter-century after him.

There were early warning signs that all was not well. When I learned, a year into my service, that a lay faculty colleague was being terminated in a manner that seemed to me highly arbitrary, I voiced my dismay to the Jesuit dean. "We'd never treat you like that, Jay," he told me. Foolishly I accepted this assurance and declined an invitation from the faculty at Leuven to return there, preferring to pursue tenure in St. Louis when I became eligible for this after two years.

By far the best theologian on the Divinity School faculty during my time there was a Dutch Jesuit: charming, a gentleman through and through, scholarly, a centrist in theology, and not an exponent of the "advanced" or left-wing views held by many of his countrymen. I was shocked to learn that the Jesuit dean of the school (who, on the testimony of his Jesuit students years before, was a mediocre teacher at best) had told his colleague in the cruelest fashion that he was incompetent and must return to Holland. In my presence this dean then informed the inter-faculty consortium, which included the two Protestant divinity schools in St. Louis, that the Dutchman, who was highly esteemed by the group, had been "recalled to Holland by his Provincial." When I visited my erstwhile colleague in Holland some years later, I found him still bitter at his treatment in St. Louis.

At the time of my first application for tenure, I had more publications than all my colleagues combined (four books and scores of articles and book reviews). The authorities were unimpressed. I was twice denied tenure, and then terminated. The only explanation given for this action was that it was "the result of long and careful deliberation, and essential for the good of the school." This institutional rescue effort came too late. The Divinity School's closure, due to falling enrollment, was announced shortly after my departure in May 1974.

When a new archbishop, John L. May, tried after his arrival in 1980 to find out the reason for my dismissal, he told me that the Jesuit chancellor of the university declined to discuss the matter. I myself asked a Jesuit at the university who remained friendly to me to give May his account of what had happened. My friend's letter made three points:

- My dismissal had nothing to do with my academic qualifications, but everything to do with personal dislike.
- I had far more publications than any of those who judged me and found me wanting.
- No one doubted that if I had been a Missouri Province Jesuit, I would have been retained and given tenure.

* * *

Many years later a layman in St. Louis who had come to know me through my writings and a lecture that I gave asked a Jesuit friend at the university whether I was a Jesuit myself.

"We wish he were," was the reply.

26

On the Scrapheap

Victims of corporate downsizing may learn when they come into the office in the morning that they must clean out their desks and be gone within the hour. I experienced no such trauma. I saw the walls closing in long before. The news came to me in a late-night phone call from my department chairman. He told me that the dean would inform me the next day that I was being terminated. To avoid having this stigma on my *curriculum vitae*, I could resign. He strongly urged me to do so. I recognized the good intention behind this advice. But I declined to accept it.

"I agree with you about the stigma, Dick," I told him. "But it doesn't attach to me. The dean will have to do his dirty work himself."

Early the next morning, I opened the Breviary (the book of prayers, psalms, and readings from Scripture and the saints, which the church asks priests to pray daily). It was the second

Tuesday in the four-week Breviary cycle. The first words I saw were:

"Commit your life to the Lord, and he will act on your behalf."

It was as if the Lord were speaking to me personally, reassuring me: "Don't worry, Jay. Trust me. I'm looking after you."

The words of Psalm 36, which followed, deepened this message:

> Be still before the Lord and wait in patience; do not fret, it only leads to evil... A little longer, and the wicked shall have gone. But the humble shall own the land, and enjoy the fullness of peace.

Had I known that the psalmist's "little longer" would stretch to seven long and lonely years of unemployment, the feeling of confidence these words gave me would have vanished. The Lord in his mercy and wisdom does not tell us these things in advance. In the years following, however, I found that a number of life crises, such as major surgery, fell on a second Tuesday in the Breviary cycle. Each time the words of the day's first psalm renewed my confidence that I was in God's loving care.

* * *

I needed all the reassurance I could get. Over the next several years I applied for over a hundred vacancies clear around the world. I had a few interviews, but no job offers. Having done my doctorate in Germany, I was not connected to any "Old Boy Network" at American universities. With four books in print and more on the way, I was overqualified for a junior appointment (assistant professor). And as a Church historian I was considered an outsider by the theologians and historians alike—too much the historian for the former, too theological for the latter.

I lived, as I had since November 1970, in a modest house provided for me by some fine Catholic Sisters near the nursing home they run. Though not their chaplain (a succession of other priests held that position during my seventeen years there), I celebrated a daily Mass for the Sisters and gave them a monthly conference. For these modest services I received room, board, and laundry, but no stipend.

I suffered no physical privation, but the blow to my self-esteem was great. In what should have been the best years of my life (from age 46 to 53), I was on the scrapheap. Several times I offered myself to the local archbishop, Cardinal Carberry. He overflowed with courtesy, but could see no way of inserting me into a system that works basically by seniority without upsetting the whole pecking order. Since my ecclesiastical superior was still the bishop of Münster, I was like an army officer who got detached from his regiment. The system did not know what to do with me.

How grateful I was to the Sisters who provided me with a home. With the top-heavy title, "Sisters of St. Francis of the Martyr St. George," they had come to St. Louis from Germany in the early 1920s. The older Sisters were almost all German, with names like characters in a Wagner opera: Adeltrudis, Ingeborg, Adelgundis, Giselberta, Guntilda, Walburga.

What magnificent women they were: stalwart in faith, persevering and never giving up despite all difficulties and obstacles. One of them, a slight figure who stood all day in the kitchen with high laced boots to support weak ankles, told me that she had come from Germany a half century before to nurse the sick. Her superiors put her in the kitchen instead.

"*Das war sehr schwer* (That was very hard)," was her only comment. She said this with no trace of regret or bitterness. She radiated peace and joy. I often saw her kneeling in the chapel, bolt upright, without support, her two thin arms raised in prayer for long periods in a posture of surrender. How happy she was, and we for her, when she was called back, at age eighty, to her order's mother house across the Mississippi River in Alton, Illinois, to live out the rest of her days as an Adoration Sister.

I enjoyed speaking German with these older Sisters. Their English, in most cases, was less than perfect, and the same was true, after decades in a foreign land, of their German. Sometimes the two languages were mixed without embarrassment, as in the case of the Sister who announced one day, as she brought me breakfast after Mass:

"Ich hab my mind up-ge-maked."

Early in my time with these Sisters, one of them lay in a sickroom just beyond the chapel balcony. I would visit and pray with her in the evening, often reading her a psalm or other Scripture passage in German, thinking that she would enjoy hearing her mother tongue in the evening of her long life. Whenever I prayed the prayer before communion at Mass, "Lord, look not on our sins, but on the faith of your Church," I would think, *the faith of the Church is up there in that sick room, in the person of that Sister.*'

As I was taking my leave one evening in May, she said: "Tomorrow is Christ's Ascension. How wonderful if he would take me with him."

I agreed—more out of courtesy than conviction, for there was no indication that her death was imminent.

When I entered the sacristy for Mass before six the next morning, the sacristan told me,-"Sister died just after four this morning."

We buried her in the cemetery at the Sisters' mother house two days later. I believe she prays, even now, for the forgiveness of my sins. Such experiences are unforgettable—and for a priest, happily not rare.

In contrast to most women's orders today, these Franciscan Sisters have abundant vocations. Experiencing their joyous annual reception of novices, and of temporary and life vows from those who have entered in previous years, is like being in a time warp—a throwback to the vocational heyday of the 1950s.

My celebration of twenty-five years of priesthood in April 1979[48] afforded a welcome opportunity to pay tribute to these Sisters in their convent chapel.

> When I look back over the road I have traveled—or better, the path along which, by God's providence, I have been led—I can say with the psalmist: "The lot is fallen to me in a fair ground; yes, I have a goodly heritage" (Psalm 16:6: Book of Common Prayer).
>
> Not the smallest part of that goodly heritage for which I publicly thank God today is the privilege of living in daily contact with some of the great people of the Church in our generation. The greatest people in the Church are not necessarily those with the fancy clothes and impressive titles. The Church's truly great people are those who live closest to God and who are most

full of his love. Many of them are "little people," as the world judges these things: known only to God and the holy angels.

There are such people in this house. If I am still a priest today, if I am still trying in some measure to live up to the name and character of Christian which, like all of you, I received in baptism, it is not least because of the shining example of a few people here, older by far than I, who are brimful of the goodness and love of God, of whom it may be said, as was said once of Moses: "They endure, as seeing him who is invisible" (Hebrews 11:27).

* * *

These years on the scrapheap (as I called them at the time) produced numerous articles, both scholarly and popular. I started work on a biography of Gilbert Burnet, from 1689 until his death in 1715 Anglican Bishop of Salisbury and author of a three-volume *History of the English Reformation.* Foundation grants took me twice to England for research. But my heart was not in it. With motivation one can achieve wonders; without it, very little. Apart from voluminous notes, the only fruit of my labor was an article reporting a significant find.[49]

For three years I wrote the Sunday homilies for *The Priest* magazine.[50] I also published a dozen or more book reviews annually: in the *St. Louis Post-Dispatch* and in academic and other journals on both sides of the Atlantic. I was busy. Save for the homilies, however, it was mostly make-work. As my hope of returning to academic life faded, and finally disappeared, I drifted, like a ship without a rudder.

Worst of all was the loneliness. I lived in my little house like a Carthusian monk in his hermitage. Following six o'clock Mass with the Sisters and prayer afterward (at first twenty minutes, soon lengthened to a half hour). I would breakfast and return to my house. The rest of the day I was alone, often seeing and speaking to no one until the next morning. Even phone calls were rare. I made many efforts to reach out and seek contact with others. None were successful.

My homily at the celebration of my silver jubilee, already quoted, reflected my mood at the time. Preaching on the Gospel reading, "Launch out into the deep," I spoke about Peter's discouragement after a night of fruitless toil on the lake, the net coming back empty hour after hour, until Peter and his companions were bone weary.

> No one can reach middle life, or come (as I must be reckoned to have come) beyond life's midpoint, without experiencing weariness, discouragement, and at least the temptation to despair. There is more than one person in this chapel today who has said, with Peter in our Gospel reading: "Master, we have toiled all night and taken nothing."

How did I survive? Only by prayer. Entering the Catholic Church had been the most difficult thing I had ever done. Now that Church, seemingly, had no use for me. Was it all for naught? I could not believe that. Daily, even hourly, I offered myself to God in prayer, asking him to do for me what, quite obviously, I was unable to do myself: raise me from the pit I was in and use me for his glory.

The story of Peter's miraculous catch of fish comes twice in the Gospels, I reminded those at my anniversary celebration. In John's Gospel, I said,

> It is the risen Lord who stands on the shore at dawn and, unrecognized by Peter and his weary crew out on the lake, calls out to them to "let down the net on the starboard side" (John 21:6). In this hour the risen Lord is confronting us, weary from life's struggle, discouraged at its meager rewards. We wanted so much. We've settled for so little.
>
> "Launch out into the deep water," he is saying. "Do not abandon the quest, though it seems fruitless. Leave the shallow waters near shore, forsake what is familiar and secure for the challenge of the unknown deep. Dare, like Peter, to do the unthinkable, and like him, you too will experience the impossible."
>
> What that impossible may be, what is coming—for you, for myself, for any of us—I cannot know, save that it is certain, like the past, to contain surprises, difficulties, struggles, and trials.
>
> But *who* is coming, we do know. His name we have all received in baptism. For his service we were commissioned by the outpouring of his grace in confirmation. His mercy and healing touch we experience in the sacrament of penance. His body and blood we receive in the Eucharist. His uniform I wear with happiness and pride, though unworthy.
>
> To his service I rededicate myself today. In a world of

constant and rapid change, in which nothing is certain save change itself, he remains always the same: ever faithful, ever true.

And him I joyfully proclaim to you: "Jesus Christ, the same yesterday, today, yes and forever."[51]

27

ST. LOUIS PRIEST

"You shouldn't spend so much time with Father Hughes. You're ruining your reputation."

"My reputation? What reputation? I never *had* any reputation."

My St. Louis priest-friend Ted reported this exchange to me himself. The warning came from his aunt, who after following an older priest from assignment to assignment as the man's housekeeper, had her finger firmly on the pulse of clerical opinion.

"The priests in St. Louis are all afraid of you, Jay," Ted told me during a 1993 visit to Prague. "They think you're an egghead because you write books, because you went to Harvard, because you're smarter than they are, and smarter than the archbishop. If only they knew how crazy you really are."

The occasion of this characteristic putdown from a man who was seldom far short of outrageous was my participation in a Mass in the Prague Cathedral for the sixth centenary of the city's patron, St. John Nepomuk.[52] Cardinal Meisner of Cologne presided as the Pope's Legate, along with the Hungarian Cardinal Paskai of Esztergom and a host of other worthies. I enjoyed talking with them as we vested before the Mass, and again in the sacristy afterward. Ted watched the proceedings on television in our apartment off Wenceslaus Square, demolishing me on my return with withering scorn—always his long suit.

Ted's remarks had a pre-history—a *Vorgeschichte,* the Germans call it—which I must now relate.

* * *

Following Pope Paul VI's acceptance of Cardinal Carberry's resignation on the latter's seventy-fifth birthday in July 1979 (a blow from which Carberry never fully recovered), January 1980 brought news of a new archbishop. He was John L. May, formerly a priest and auxiliary bishop in Chicago, and for the previous decade bishop of Mobile, Alabama. Within weeks of his arrival in St. Louis, May picked me up out of the gutter with a stick and made me his personal theologian.

In the autumn of 1980 May said he would like to make me a priest of the St. Louis archdiocese. To accomplish this, I had first to be released ("excardinated" is the technical term) by the bishop of Münster. The necessary papers soon arrived, but for some time May was unable to find suitable work for me. In conversations over many weeks I told him that my incardination in St. Louis would make little sense if he had nothing meaningful for me to do.

In late February 1981 I was working in the basement office of my little house when the telephone rang. It was Archbishop

May. He wanted to make me Director of RENEW. What on earth was that, I asked? May explained that it was a program of spiritual renewal that he hoped to implement throughout the archdiocese. I recognized at once that this was the breakthrough for which I had prayed daily for seven long and lonely years. I accepted at once, with thanks. I was euphoric.

RENEW was a runaway success. Much of this was due to Fr. Bill Scheid, the younger St. Louis priest who assisted me and whom I insisted from the start be my co-director (May originally appointed him my associate). Scheid was well liked and trusted by his peers, few of whom had any idea, when I was appointed, who I was. Over 90% of our 225 parishes participated. The small faith-sharing groups that were the heart of the program enrolled over 50,000 people. That was 10% of all the baptized Catholics in the archdiocese, the highest proportion of any of the scores of dioceses in the country that implemented RENEW.

One measure of the program's success was that laypeople were still talking enthusiastically about their experience years later. Many of the priests were also appreciative. Not so, however, the movers and shakers in the diocese. The program was so successful that for its four years' duration it dwarfed all other diocesan-wide efforts. Worst of all, it was led by an outsider who, they complained, "came out of nowhere" (i.e., was neither a native St. Louisan nor an alumnus of the local seminary), and who—the crowning horror—was a convert.

As RENEW drew to a close in the autumn of 1984, we circulated a questionnaire to the priests asking for suggestions for follow up. Continuing the policy of candor that had served us well from the start, we published a sampling of these responses, including critical ones. The latter included the blunt demand: "Bury it as soon as it expires."

That was exactly what happened. RENEW was expunged, so far as this was possible, from the collective consciousness. And for over a year I was given no further assignment. While I could understand the resentment, born of envy, of fellow priests, I was taken aback when Archbishop May said to me, in one of our many fruitless conversations about my future work after RENEW's conclusion, "We never expected that RENEW was going to be so big." It was clear from the context that this was intended more as a reproach than as a compliment.

* * *

To fill the time, I started work in January 1985 on what would become my ninth book. Our Sunday Visitor, which commissioned it, published it in 1994 under the title *Pontiffs: Popes Who shaped History.*

By January 1986 I had been a full year without assignment. I informed the archbishop that if he could not use me, I intended to offer myself to a bishop who could. For six weeks I rattled my cage, telling priest-friends of my intention to leave the diocese if there was no work for me. In early March May told me that he wanted to make me vice chancellor of the archdiocese. I had already bought an air ticket to Florida, intending to offer my services to the bishops of two newly erected dioceses there, when I received this wholly unexpected proposal. It occasioned none of the euphoria I had felt when May made me Director of RENEW. I was grateful for the goodwill manifest in his proposal. But it was clear from May's description of the position that it would be little more than an empty title, with few significant duties or responsibilities. It was equally clear, however, that I could not decline.

The reality turned out to be as expected. I sat daily in a sumptuous office, signed dispensations for mixed marriages, typed the annual Diocesan Directory, and occasionally attended a meeting or luncheon as the archbishop's representative. A friendly parish pastor, visiting me one day for my signature on a marriage dispensation (he is bishop of another diocese today), told me, "Jay, you're like a brain surgeon who has been told he can only give out Band-Aids."

The job had one duty that, though not always pleasant, was sometimes amusing: receiving telephone calls of complaints, often about my fellow priests. I always tried to listen to the caller, to avoid being defensive, and to suggest possible reasons for the priest's action, or extenuating circumstances. Whenever possible, I urged the caller to take the matter up with the priest directly, in a personal conversation and not with a letter or phone call.

I regret now that I did not keep a record of some of these complaints. Some would have been welcome additions to my file of "Nuts, cranks, crackpots, and screwballs." Clearly in that category was the woman who asked me on the phone one day, "Father, do you realize that there are priests in this archdiocese who are telling people that Jesus had body odor? They're even telling them that Mary had body odor. Now, Father, Jesus maybe. But Our Lady? No way."

It was clearly not a teaching moment. I thanked the lady for her concern.

* * *

On more than one occasion I added to the archbishop's burdens by telling him of my frustration. He assured me each time that he intended to give me a parish. In January 1988 he did so. The place to which he was sending me, a bedroom community for St. Louis, had been described to me by a priest who had served there previously as "a redneck community." I recognized at once that I was utterly unqualified for the position. Accepting it cost me a bitter inner struggle. Within twenty-four hours of doing so, I was in a hospital emergency room with a painful inflammation of the eye. I have no doubt that the cause was psychosomatic: the body's rebellion against severe mental stress.

I threw myself into this new work with determination. Using the stewardship principles I had learned in Utica over three decades before, I was able to increase the parish income by 50% in one year. Financial contributions are no measure of spiritual success. But increased giving is unlikely if people reject their pastor.

A determined minority did so, however, from the start. The parish had a century-and-a-half history, old for the American Midwest. With countless inter-marriages, and private feuds too tangled for an outsider to unravel, a core of lifelong parishioners regarded the parish as their private club, to which priests were admitted as long as they did as they were told. Those who did not were run out of town and replaced. Six weeks after my arrival, I learned that this had happened to my predecessor. When I reproached the archbishop for sending me into an active minefield with no warning, he responded, "I thought you knew."

An incident in a parish council meeting was typical. A

young woman, expressing disagreement with a decision I had made, said angrily:

"But, Father, it's *our* parish."

"No, Mary," I countered. "It is not your parish. And it is certainly not my parish. It is the Lord's parish. We all serve him."

Jaws dropped all around the table. No one had ever spoken to them like that before. A month later, when tempers had cooled, I told the council,

"When we met around this table a month ago, we were told: 'It's our parish.' If the 'our' in that statement includes all of us, priest and people together, then I affirm the statement a hundred times. But that was not what we were being told. What was really meant was, 'It is our parish, Father, and not yours. And if you don't do what we want, we're going to run you out of town, like we ran off the last pastor, and get someone else.'"

The troublemakers were a heavy burden. But there were others (there always are, in every parish) whom it was a privilege to serve: people totally devoted to the Lord and his Church and warmly supportive of their priests. I think especially of two men who gave hours of their time every Saturday to working around the church and grounds. It was typical of their dedication that, on the evening of my farewell as pastor, they excused themselves immediately after Mass, missing the reception in order to put the rectory in order to receive my successor the next day.

In twenty-one months in that parish I did not have a single happy day. I was astonished, therefore, to learn years later, from a St. Louis priest then in Rome, that an auxiliary bishop with relatives in the parish had told him that I had been "a superb pastor." I thought I had been competent, but nothing more.

* * *

My next assignment came as a complete surprise. Though priests hostile to me had told people in the parish that I had asked for it, the truth is that I knew so little about the place that I had to ask directions to find it on my initial visit. It was in affluent exurbia. Horses and the white fences enclosing them were prominent features of the landscape. Most of the bathtubs within the parish boundaries were furnished with underwater jets and could accommodate two people.

The parish had been founded eleven years previously and had known only one pastor. A devoted and zealous priest, he did not have "No" in his vocabulary. This failing, common among the clergy, arises from the misconception that, as members of a helping profession, we must never offend anyone. The effort to please everyone had sent my predecessor to the hospital with a bleeding ulcer.

The man was greatly beloved, and deservedly so. The announcement that he was being moved to another parish provoked a firestorm of indignation. I learned of this when I visited the archbishop to discuss my new charge. He confronted me with a thick stack of petitions protesting the removal of the founding pastor, implying that they were somehow my fault. Instead of assuring me of his support, and counseling me how to proceed in a volatile situation, he warned sternly that if I did not proceed with the utmost caution, he would have to remove me. Had he set out to destabilize me, he could hardly have achieved his objective more effectively.

I was happy in the parish nonetheless. Trouble came from a quarter that has proved the undoing of many pastors: church furnishings. The building had been built cheaply in contemporary style—nice enough outside, but poorly designed within. The worst defect was the placement of the altar: in the lowest corner of a church with a steeply slanting roof. As a result, the sanctuary, which could have had height and dignity, had the interior been differently arranged, was cramped. An engineer in the parish pointed out that the principal roof beam did not rest on the column designed to carry it. The church furnishings (candlesticks, crucifix, etc.) were tasteless commercial productions, as in so many American churches.

After having seen in Europe so many beautiful churches, old and new, I was aware of these defects at once. At the same time, I realized that I must move slowly. I resolved to do nothing for a full year while people got to know and trust me. Meanwhile I started building up a fund for church renovation, from special gifts.

On a bicycle trip in Vermont toward the end of my first year in the parish, I discovered, in a tiny Benedictine priory, a modern crucifix of striking beauty. The corpus was stiff and stylized, like a Byzantine icon. It was a copy of a crucifix made for Pope Paul VI, who used it on the altar erected for Mass in St. Peter's Square. The only other copy hung over the high altar at the Benedictine Abbey in Portsmouth, Rhode Island. I obtained permission to have it copied. Set on a processional cross of wrought iron, I placed it next to the free-standing altar in the church. The craftsman who made it also fashioned a wrought iron candelabra, which I placed on the other side of the altar, replacing the conventional and uninspired candlesticks that had previously stood on the altar itself.

Working closely with a gifted architect who had already supervised the renovation of a number or St. Louis churches, I completed these embellishments by having eighteen inches cut off each end of the stone table-altar, which was grossly overproportioned for the space. I covered the altar with a rich tapestry of modern design (to match the church), which hung to the floor on all sides. I informed the parish council, and parishioners through the Sunday bulletin, that all this had been paid for from special gifts, not with the regular Sunday offerings. For these changes I received a number of compliments and one letter of angry complaint.

Storm clouds gathered, however, when I showed people the architect's sketch for further modification of the sanctuary. In a meeting of the parish council one of my strongest supporters hitherto reversed field, declaring that the proposed plan was "a hard sell." A married couple of great wealth warned me that if I proceeded further, it would "split the parish."

The renovations I was proposing were quite modest. (We could not afford more.) They were the result of expert advice. Though no artist myself, I had seen the best and knew the difference between beauty and kitsch. If people preferred the latter, I had no heart to fight them.

Then something else happened.

In July 1990 I learned that I had prostate cancer.

* * *

My prostate was removed on September 17, 1990. It was several weeks before I was back in the parish. For four months thereafter I had to wear a pad and was wet at the altar and in the pulpit. In January 1991 I had further surgery, to correct a hernia. In Holy Week I was hospitalized yet again with acute influenza. Health problems of this magnitude forced me to consider whether it was prudent to continue as pastor.

With great kindness, for I had often been a trial to him, Archbishop May offered me lighter duties as theological consultant in the archdiocese. My initial task would be to prepare a collection of his writings to be published on his twenty-fifth anniversary as a bishop in 1992. My salary would be paid by the diocese,[53] and I could live in any rectory I chose.

I hesitated for many weeks to accept this offer. Giving up my parish was a gamble. A pastor has, in canon law, a more secure position than priests in other assignments. For a number of Sundays I looked out on the hundreds of people in the crowded church, sensing their loyalty and affection, and asked myself, *Do I really want to walk away from all this?*

A younger priest who had helped me greatly with his wise counsel in several past perplexities clarified the decision for me with a single challenging question: "Jay, do you want to be pastor of that parish in five years?"

My answer came at once: "I do not."

A parish pastorate, I realized in that moment, had never been for me the defining role that it is for most diocesan priests. I had worked hard in both my parishes and had done well. But I was doing the job with my left hand. My real interests lay elsewhere: in following developments in the Church, here and overseas, through reading and a large correspondence, and in my writing, especially the ongoing work on the book *Pontiffs,* then nearing completion.

In the letter to parishioners announcing my resignation, I said:

> When I told you just a year ago that I had cancer, I said: "We priests preach trust in God in difficult times. It is only right that we should have an opportunity to exercise that trust ourselves." Today I recall something in a little book of "Principles" given to me when I entered seminary forty-three years ago: "You should have nothing you cannot easily lay aside. You must leave all one day, whether you will or not."
>
> I lay down the burden of pastoral leadership in that spirit. I cannot think of a better preparation for the Great Farewell that awaits us all at life's end: the journey home to God.

* * *

Difficult as the decision to resign the parish was, I experienced an immediate lifting of spirits as soon as I left. A year later I wrote in my report for the forty-fifth reunion of my Harvard class:

> In August 1991 I resigned the nicest parish I could ever have been given in the St. Louis archdiocese to accept the position of archdiocesan theological consultant offered me by Archbishop John L. May. I have not regretted it for a single minute. I have now produced a 350-page collection of the archbishop's writings, to be published in the autumn of 1992, in connection with his celebration of twenty-five years as a bishop. I have also worked at my own writing: book reviews

for the *St. Louis Post-Dispatch* and scholarly journals, and completion of my ninth book, *Pontiffs: Popes Who Shaped History.*

I live in a quiet, comfortable rectory and assist the pastor (a former student and longtime friend) in his small parish. Forest Park, larger than New York's Central Park, is two miles distant. My daily bicycle ride around it is eleven miles door to door. I greatly enjoy the freedom from parish administration and the leisure for reading, writing, and travel. On New Year's Day 1992 I was off Cape Horn on a small Italian cruise ship with my remarkable eighty-nine-years-young stepmother. And I have just returned from sailing with friends in the Virgin Islands, where my younger brother, having completed a circumnavigation under sail in his own boat, is now assistant attorney general on St. Croix. September 1992 will see me sailing through the Greek islands with a priest-friend. Life is good, and I am grateful.

The late German theologian, Karl Rahner, under whom I studied in Innsbruck and Münster, wrote before his death in 1984 that we were going through "a wintry time" in the Catholic Church. Spring will come again: it always does, in the Church as in nature. Whether I shall experience it depends on how many years remain to me.

The escalation of expectations weighs heavily on all the professions. I found this documented for surgeons in a book by the St. Louisan Joan Cassell aptly entitled *Expected Miracles.* Reviewing the book in the *Post-Dispatch*, I quoted "an exasperated fellow priest" (myself) saying: "They expect us to be perfect. People who don't begin to approach perfection themselves won't accept us as ordinary, flawed sinners like themselves." I love the priesthood more than ever. But I have no taste for much of parish life: the endless meetings, complaints, gossip, bickering, and constant petty and not-so-petty attacks. Who needs it?

Following surgery for prostate cancer in September 1990, my health is robust, my spirits higher than they have been for years. In sum, I am happy, fulfilled, and at peace.

* * *

In July 1992 Archbishop May underwent surgery for a cancer far more virulent than mine: a tumor on the brain. He was a pathetic shadow of his formerly vigorous self when I gave him the first copy of his book that autumn.[54] It was an attractive volume, embellished with twenty-five photographs. The Catholic Press Association gave the book an award that year.

Like many strong men in leadership positions, May did not find it easy to bestow praise. I was greatly moved, therefore, when he telephoned me many weeks after receiving his copy of the book to say, in the painfully slow, almost slurred speech that resulted from his heavy medication, "Jay, your work is *superb.*"

From May, that was high praise indeed.

He died on March 24, 1994, a day short of fourteen years from the date of his installation as archbishop of St. Louis. We shall meet again in heaven.

28

"Her Mouth Was Filled with Laughter . . ."

My remarkable eighty-nine-years-young stepmother, as I called her in the 1993 report for my Harvard class, played a central role in my life for the better part of two decades. Following my father's death in 1964, she lived on, independently and alone, in the house he had left her in Newport, Rhode Island. I was able to visit her only infrequently. But starting in the mid-1980s we traveled together all over the world: throughout North America, but also to Europe, Central and South America, New Zealand and Australia, and Southeast Asia. For many years I telephoned her daily to chat, and also to laugh. That was what Bina did best.

At the end of October 1996, surgery disclosed that Bina had pancreatic cancer. I was with her at the time and for a week thereafter. By mid-November she was back in the home she loved, and which reflected her personality. Nurses and family members cared for her lovingly.

In the first week of 1997, I learned through telephone calls that Bina was nearing the end of her long life.

"She's just waiting for you, Jay," I was told.

I reached Newport the evening of Tuesday, January 7, and anointed her the next day. She lingered until Friday when, at two thirty in the afternoon, her breathing became labored. My sister-in-law Rosamond and I kept vigil at the bedside as afternoon turned to evening. Rosamond had accompanied Bina on a trip to Europe the previous May. She had promised Bina that when the time came, she would be with her to the end. Now she was fulfilling that pledge—a joy to Rosamond, and surely to Bina as well.

Anointing may be repeated if the sick person has a fresh crisis. So at a quarter to eight in the evening, I anointed Bina again. As soon as I had done so, I bent over her and said, as lovingly as I could, "Bina, dear, you have given so much joy and laughter to so many. You can go now, to be with the Lord, and with Daddy."

There was no response. But all the literature about dying says that hearing is the last faculty to be lost. I am confident that she heard and understood.

At 8:31 Bina quietly took her last breath, squeezing Rosamond's hand in farewell just before she did so. She was in her ninety-fourth year.

How can one grieve at such a death? Her funeral on January 18, in my father's old church, St. Columba's in Middletown, was a grateful celebration of her magnificent, long life. My own contribution had been prepared long before. Its delivery was no less heartfelt for that.

On the twenty-fourth of May 1903, Corinna Putnam, a daughter of the Boston publishing family and married to the American artist and Egyptologist Joseph Lindon Smith, was delivered in a London lodging house of a baby girl, her second child and daughter. "Your baby's come," the midwife called downstairs to the father, "and she's a tiny." She would receive the name Frances in baptism. But Tiny she would remain to family and friends until, some years later, her younger sister Lois announced that everyone in the family must have a name beginning with B. Her father became Buzzer, her mother Bummer, the first-born Rebecca became Becky, and Tiny became Bina, the name by which most of us here knew her.

To childhood friends she remained Tiny, however, a name which she considered inappropriate, she said in recent years, "now that I've become a fat old lady." "Fat" was an exaggeration. But no one could dispute that, in her tenth decade, Bina was old. In spirit, however, she remained youthful to the end, with all her marbles, including not a few that she picked up from inattentive players whom she encountered along life's way.

Bina grew up in the shadow of a glamorous eighteen-months-older sister and the forceful personality of her strong-willed mother. She was especially close to her father, who in addition to being an artist, was also a gifted amateur actor and stage director and, beyond question, the funniest man I have ever known. Bina inherited a full share of her father's humor.

It was not just her humor, however, that was responsible for the laughter that all who encountered her noticed immediately. For the truth (unperceived by most, for it was well concealed) was that Bina was painfully shy. Her laughter, often unprovoked and inappropriate, resulted as often from embarrassment as it did from humor.

In her childhood and teens, Bina joined her parents on her father's painting expeditions to distant parts of the world. In the unending flow of anecdote and reminiscence, which was, after her laugh, her most characteristic feature, she loved to tell of living on a houseboat on the Nile while her father painted objects from the nearby tombs. She was thrilled to discover, only last year, old photographs from this period, showing her and her sister Becky with the ingenious toys fashioned for them by the family's Egyptian servants.

Despite these adventures, Bina's youth was far from idyllic. She hated the boarding school to which she was sent in her teens. And her shyness was no match for her hard-driving mother and her beautiful older sister. Her father sympathized and did what he could. But an artist's life is necessarily solitary. Bina must often have felt in her youth that the name by which she was first known, Tiny, fitted her just right.

From this oppressive atmosphere she was rescued, in her mid-twenties, by the Yale graduate, Raymond

Otis. A writer in rebellion against his conventional upbringing, he carried Bina off to Santa Fe, where the couple joined eagerly in the Bohemian life of the colony of artists and writers attracted by the unique combination of cultures—Hispanic, Indian, and American—the clear light of the desert, and the beauty of the surrounding mountains. It was a wonderfully happy marriage, filled with laughter and fun, though never blessed with children. It would last ten years only. Ray Otis died in 1938, leaving Bina a widow at thirty-five.

Not quite three years later, Bina met my father, himself a widower since the death of my mother in 1934. Within weeks, they were engaged. That was in February 1941. I was only twelve. I can still remember, as if it were yesterday, how much younger my father seemed. For the first time I realized how lonely he had been since my mother's death.

My sister Jane and my brother Dudley will surely confirm that we grew up no strangers to humor and laughter. Bina bought us, however, a kind of fey humor (inherited from her father), which was new to us. There can be few people here without their own examples of Bina's humor. From my own collection let me give you just one.

On a trip to Ireland in 1990, she complained that I ate and slept to excess. "You eat these enormous meals, and then sleep your life away," she said. "You're like a boa constrictor." As I collapsed into helpless laughter, Bina had the last word (she liked the last word): "Well, that's what they do."

* * *

Some of you may have wondered at the choice of the Gospel reading we heard a few moments ago: the great parable of judgment, the story of the sheep and the goats. It was chosen quite deliberately. A striking feature of the story is the surprise of those praised for their good deeds.

"Lord, when did we see you hungry and feed you, or see you thirsty and give you to drink?" those on the King's right hand ask. "When did we welcome you away from home or clothe you in your nakedness? When did we visit you when you were ill or in prison?" They don't recall having done anything special or exceptional.

Bina was like that. As the shadows of her remarkable long life lengthened, she often expressed surprise at how good people were to her. When the conversation would turn, for instance, to unhappy or broken marriages, she would say, "Well, I was just lucky to have had two husbands who were very good to me and looked after me." It never occurred to Bina that other people's kindness had anything at all to do with her. She thought it was just luck, just the way the numbers came up. Those of us who loved Bina—and there can be few people who knew her who did not love her—know that in this at least she was mistaken.

In a late-night conversation many years ago at Loon Point, her parents' summer place in Dublin, New Hampshire, Bina and I spoke of things we regretted. "I think I regret most the things I *haven't* done," Bina said to me. That too fits our Gospel reading. For those at the King's left hand in the story are condemned not for what they have done, but for things left undone.

In the last two decades I traveled often with Bina, to the far corners of the world. I trudged with her up a mountain in Switzerland, where she twisted an ankle and refused to see a doctor until she got home, because (as she said later when the X-ray showed a cracked bone), "I was afraid he would tell me to stay off my feet." I stood with her atop a mountain in New Zealand, where she raised a clenched fist in triumph as I snapped her picture. I stood with her on the heaving deck of a small ship a mile off Cape Horn. Only months before her ninetieth birthday, she rode behind me on a jet ski off a beach in Malaysia, and on an elephant in Bangkok.

Not one single night in all these travels did Bina get into bed without kneeling to pray. She knew that without a power greater than her own, she could never master life's difficulties. This unobtrusive, well-concealed, but rock-like faith was what gave Bina the strength to live, as it has now given her the courage to face death with cheerfulness and grace. It was her faith in our all-powerful and loving heavenly Father that enabled Bina, in a telephone conversation with me in early November only hours after being told that she had pancreatic cancer, to say: "I feel like the English poet Alan Seeger, who wrote:

'I have a rendezvous with Death at some disputed barricade.'"

She went on to quote some more lines from the poet and to tell of his visit to her family at Loon Point, and of his death in the First World War. That from a terminally ill cancer patient in her ninety-fourth year. She was a woman of faith. And she certainly had all her marbles.

Now Bina has gone to the source of that light that she has handed on to us to be kept burning brightly. "I can see, I can see!" Bina exclaimed when the bandages were removed after a delicate and successful operation on her one remaining good eye in St. Louis a few years ago. The new and clearer vision that was given to her that day, however, is as nothing compared to the clarity with which Bina now sees. After a wonderful long life, God has called her home: where sight is clouded no longer; where there are no endless nights of waiting for the dawn; where there is no more sadness, no more sorrow, no more loneliness, no more misunderstanding, no more weakness, sickness, or pain; where Bina, as we confidently pray, will experience ecstasy—when she sees God face to face.

* * *

> That, my dears, is my message to you. Allow me, if you will, a final personal word to Bina.
>
> In the wonderful speech you read to us at the celebration of your ninetieth birthday, Bina, you said, "My life has been a mixed bag and a somewhat winding road. I have always had an insatiable curiosity to see what's around that next corner. I've had some wonderful surprises for which I'm grateful, and some sad ones ... but you have to keep moving. There is always another corner until the final one."
>
> You certainly did keep moving, Bina. Often, however, when I was driving you, you would fall asleep, missing the magnificent scenery through which we traveled. When we got to our destination, I would say: "Bina, we're here. We've arrived!"
>
> It has been a wonderful, long journey. I count it among the greatest blessings of a richly blessed life to have made so much of the journey with you. Now, Bina, you have turned that final corner. And so I say to you once, again: "Bina! You're home. You're home!"[55]

* * *

We buried her in the churchyard of St. Columba's under a flat stone of Rhode Island slate with an inscription suggested by my brother, Dudley:

Frances Lindon Smith Otis Hughes 1903–1997

"Her mouth was filled with laughter,

and her tongue with joy." (Psalm 126, vs. 2).

Next to it is my father's matching stone with a carved wolf's head, from the arms of his mother's family, the Foulkes. At his request it has neither name nor dates, simply the words:

Pray for a priest whose body lies here.[56]

29

Letters to the Dead

Dear Mummy:

The little boy you last saw and waved at through the isinglass windows of your oxygen tent just before Christmas 1934 is nearing eighty now. An old man? I don't feel old. And friends tell me I don't look my age.

Would you recognize me? Of course you would. We have never been far apart. Daddy told me a few days after we buried you that we should still pray for you. I have done so faithfully all down the years. I never stand at the altar without thinking of you and praying for you by name. I know you have done the same for me.

Your death left a wound in me that has never fully healed: a void in the heart, sometimes painful, sometimes not, but always there. Why did I never marry? For years I expected to. The reason, I believe, is connected with your death. The woman I loved most dearly left me. In my subconscious I have never dared to give myself completely to another, for fear that she might leave me too. And because you died so early, my picture of women is idealized. No wife could possibly have equaled the child's memory I have of you. Had I married, my wife and I would have been in for difficult times.

From time to time, well-meaning people have suggested that I "forgive you" for leaving me. There is nothing to forgive. How can one forgive something that neither of us ever wanted?

In the years after your death I used to feel closest to you when I sat alone by the sea. Now I feel closest when I stand at the altar. It is there that I come closest to God. And you are with God.

Loneliness has been my companion for much of my life. At Kelham, in my early twenties (a time of intense loneliness), I read something that helped me:

> Turn your loneliness into solitude,
>
> which is the loveliness of being alone with God.

I have tried to do that—with growing success. In doing so I have made a wonderful discovery: the God whom I encounter in solitude fills my emptiness as no human being ever could.

Married people are lonely too. I discovered that years ago. So I have no regrets at not having married. And though I rejoice in children, and am now "Grandpa Jay" to a beguiling three-year-old whom I first saw an hour after her birth, I cannot once recall wanting children of my own.

If we could meet, you would not find me sad or depressed. You would be struck, I think, by my inner joy and peace.

If we could meet? But of course we *shall* meet! I know that.

I look forward to it. It is part, an essential part, of the Christian hope that sustains and nurtures me.

In that hope, and in gratitude for the love you gave me so generously for six and a half years, and which you have never ceased to give from beyond the grave through your prayers, I am happy to sign myself,

Your devoted and loving son,

Jay

* * *

Dear Daddy:

We hurt each other. You know how deeply I regret that. You regret it too, I know.

I tried for years to understand why you took my decision about the Church so hard. I asked your friend T.S. Matthews about it once. I could understand your being disappointed and hurt, I told him. But why did you feel it necessary to banish me from your home?

"I didn't really know him that well, Jay," he told me with more than a trace of irritation.

If he doesn't have an answer, I thought to myself, I'll never get an answer—at least not in this life—and in heaven it won't make any difference. I continued to search for an answer nonetheless. I think now that I can see at least a partial explanation.

Your mother's sister, Aunt May, a Quaker and a woman of incandescent goodness, said to me some years after your death: "Thy father was a complicated man. He had a stern side and a golden side. Thee got both, Jay." Aunt May was right.

Your sternness was not just with others. You were stern with yourself. I recognized that years ago. Recently, however, a priest-friend who was close to you during your final illness told me something I had not known before. Mindful of the mounting medical problems that had beset you for more than a year, this friend urged you to go to a research hospital in Boston for surgery rather than to the local hospital in Newport. You would get better care. Brother Dudley seconded this advice.

You brushed the suggestion aside, not as beneath contempt, but as worthy of contempt.

"No, the surgeon here needs the experience," you said. And that was that.

The possibility that acquiring that experience might result in your death—and did—was, to you, irrelevant. I am not arguing, of course, that the outcome would have been different if you had placed yourself in more expert hands. We cannot know that. I cite this incident merely as an example of your sternness with yourself.

There was nothing inconsistent, therefore, in showing this same sternness toward your eldest son, whom you loved so dearly, and of whom you had hopes so high that their fulfillment would have required a moral miracle.

Recently I read in Roy Jenkins' superb biography of the nineteenth-century English Prime Minister William Gladstone (a book you would have loved, incidentally) an account of Gladstone's attitude toward his sister Helen's conversion to the Roman Catholic Church, which struck me as remarkably familiar.

> Gladstone took Helen's move as a major family scandal and a direct personal affront... He regarded himself as

> in charge of family discipline on religious matters... He might well have seen in Helen something of his own susceptibility to temptations. Furthermore he always felt a special responsibility for defending the narrow and crucial line between his own High Anglicanism and what he regarded as the insinuating indulgences of the Church of Rome. He was therefore in favor of the most unforgiving sanctions.[57]

When I read that, it seemed an almost exact description of your attitude toward me. Scarcely a word need be changed. But that is all behind us now, thank God.

I recall listening, when I was scarcely into my teens, to one of your long conversations with fellow clergy that used to fascinate me so. Speaking of the Roman Catholic Church, you said, in a tone which suggested both prescience and omniscience, "Ah, there's a big change coming."

I haven't a clue what kind of change you had in mind. I'm not sure you did either. But you were right nonetheless. You would not approve of all the changes in the Catholic Church. But many, I am confident, would find your approval and even your gratitude.

I cannot close this long letter, Daddy, without telling you how deeply grateful I am, and have been all my life long, for all you gave me. Your endlessly fascinating conversation—pursuing every side issue, leaving no stone unturned—gave me the love of language that has brought me success as an author and preacher. You made me laugh—and still do. You taught me to love music and song. You taught me to sail. I think of you every time I put to sea, and always with gratitude and affection. And you gave us Bina.

Her marriage to you lasted twenty-three years, her widowhood thirty-three. When you married her, you never imagined, nor did she or any of us, that she would spend so much time, as a widow, with your beloved eldest son. What an enrichment that was for both of us.

The most important thing you gave me, of course, was my religious faith. Without that I could never have survived. In that faith, and in the love of the Lord who, as Paul tells us in that magnificent eighth chapter of Romans, "makes all things work together for good for those who love God," I am happy to sign myself

Your loving, devoted, and deeply grateful son,
Jay

30

ALL I EVER WANTED

"Why, then, did you become a priest?" My friend, a priest who has spent his entire life in parish ministry, could not understand how I could leave my pastorate to accept a non-parochial assignment. Challenged to say why I had become a priest, I knew the answer at once.

"I became a priest," I replied without hesitation, "so that I could celebrate Mass."

Celebrating Mass brought me joy the first time I did it fifty-four years ago. The joy is undiminished today.

The rite I use today lacks the literary beauty of the Book of Common Prayer, which shaped my liturgical taste in my youth. The English Catholic, Ann Wroe, writes:

> The English of the modern Mass has no artifice, no rhythm, no conscious beauty; like a plain stone or a white wall, it gains whatever weight or meaning we wish to give it.

Quite so. Before I approach the altar each morning, I sit quite still for a full half hour, repeating throughout the entire time the prayer-word *Maranatha*.[58] I learned this form of prayer over two decades ago from the writings and tapes of the late Anglo-Irish Benedictine, John Main. His disciple Lawrence Freeman continues his work today, worldwide.

I have written already of struggling as a young teenager with discursive meditation: using the imagination to picture a biblical scene, the mind to reflect on its meaning, and the will to make acts of faith, hope, love, repentance, and thanksgiving. By age twenty, when I entered seminary, discursive meditation gave way to spiritual reading and reflection—and as the years went by, more and more to what the books call "affective prayer." "Don't let me get away, Lord," I would pray over and over again; or "Not what I want, Lord, but what you want."

Around 1980 the American Trappist, Basil Pennington, taught me the method of centering prayer. In 1981 I published a booklet about it, mostly cribbed from Pennington and his fellow Trappist Thomas Keating. It remained in print for twenty-five years and sold almost 200,000 copies—a sign of today's deep spiritual hunger.[59] I moved on from centering prayer to Main's prayer of the mantra a few years later.

Years ago I had difficulty spending twenty minutes in silence before the Lord. Now the entire half hour often seems too short. I am disappointed when I hear the deacon preparing for Mass in the sacristy and know I must break off. A married man with a devoted wife and a host of grandchildren, he likes to chat before Mass. I don't. I am too full of what I have just been doing, and the even greater thing I am about to do.

"Put off the shoes from your feet," the Lord said to Moses

at the burning bush, "for the place where you stand is holy ground" (Exodus 3:5). None of us is worthy to enter the presence of the all-holy God. Hence the threefold prayer for mercy at the beginning of every Mass.

I listen closely to the reading (two on Sundays) and to the Gospel. If the deacon is not present, I read it myself. Then, with all the conviction and fervor at my command, I proclaim the love that will never let us go: briefly on weekdays, and at greater length and from a full manuscript on Sundays.

My appreciation of the liturgy of the word has grown over the years. When Vatican II spoke about "the table of the world," it was not only acknowledging a central postulate of the Reformation. It was also resurrecting ancient Catholic terminology. At the beginning of every council session, the book of God's Word, not the monstrance with the consecrated host, was enthroned on the altar: a reminder to those present that everything they said and did stood under the judgment of God's Word.

The Eucharistic prayer remains for me, however, the heart of the Mass. Seldom do I fail to be moved by the narrative of institution with the words of the Lord himself, "This is my body," and "This is my blood," which fascinated even Martin Luther.[60] I recite the words slowly, with reverence and awe, slightly bent over paten and chalice, as the rubrics direct.

Does this help anyone? I cannot say. I know it nourishes me. No man ever longed more ardently for the arms of his beloved than I for that daily encounter with the Lord. Those precious moments with him, repeating his words, are quite literally the high point of my day. I recall them as I write these lines. I look forward to their repetition tomorrow.

How moving to read the words of an English priest, Fr. Hugh Lavery, on his fiftieth anniversary of priesthood:

> I was new to priesthood when a wise old canon told me that the influence that most moved the people to sanctity was how Mass was said. People need the Mass as they need food and affection. A liturgy which has aptness, form, and reverence at the close makes real the presence of the Holy.[61]

Where in all this are the people for whom the priest is ordained, to whom he is supposed to minister? Those were the questions that prompted my friend's challenge: "Why, then, did you become a priest?" He could not understand a priest being satisfied without full-time pastoral ministry. This is what nourishes him. He assumed that it must nourish me too. It does not—or at least not to the same extent.

I became a priest not to be with people, but to be, in a specially intimate way, with the Lord. I honor priests who experience this intimacy through pastoral ministry. I consider them my superiors: better priests, and better human beings. I experience intimacy with the Lord most of all at the altar. Ministering to people can be fulfilling, but also frustrating. Not everyone wants what the priest has to offer. God always wants us. The worship I offer him at the altar is imperfect. Yet he never spurns it. And, for me, the offering of that worship never palls.

* * *

"I go into the confessional now," a newly ordained priest in his first parish wrote to a friend still in seminary, "and experience God in a completely new way." A priest must speak of those experiences with care. The seal of the confessional forbids us to disclose what we hear there. What I write, therefore, is anonymous. Save for the first instance, which is long ago and far away, the sins mentioned are generic rather than specific; the identity of those who confessed them unknown, even to me.

"I stamp my foot at my mother and say no." I was not more than twenty-five when I heard a child say that. Was it a sin at all? When you're only seven or eight, it is a sin. What struck me most, however, was the earnestness in the voice. *That little one has more sorrow for that small sin,* I thought, *than I do for my sins, which are far worse.* I believe the Lord sent that child into my confessional to teach me a lesson. I have never forgotten it.

Children's confessions are tedious. To sit listening for an hour or more to the same banal list of transgressions is as wearying as anything I know. Yet one must remain alert, for occasionally there is something that signals a need for help.

"You just have to accept it as a penance," a fine younger priest said to me after we had each spent ninety minutes with the school children. He was right.

Many children don't know what to say and must be prompted.

"All right, son. What are the things you want to tell Jesus you're sorry for?"

"*Oh* boy!" the youngster replies.

He has no more to say than the twenty-five who have preceded him.

Not so the next one. He goes on and on. The whole of his young life unfolds before me in rich, vivid colors, everything he has been up to for the last week at least. There is talk of snowball fights, snowmen, igloos, and sneak attacks on the igloos and snowmen of others. (Is that one of his sins? I cannot tell.) Clearly, I muse, here is a fellow human who is tasting life to the full. And at only ten!

Still this riot of hyperbole goes on, getting more and more carried away as his whole adventurous past unrolls like a tapestry before him. I have long since lost the thread of the narrative. I want to interrupt and tell him, "Enough already!" I cannot. I am laughing—and hoping he won't notice. Of course he doesn't. The lad is a genius. I want to tell him, "Son, you should get that down on paper. Write a short story, a novel. There's a market for that kind of thing."

Finally he runs down. Silence descends upon us.

"Is that all?" I ask. (*What a damn fool question,* I think. *Do you want to get him started again?*)

"Yes," he replies.

(*I was lucky that time,* I think. *Ah well, you have to have some luck—in this game as in any other.*)

"Son," I tell him, "Jesus loved you when you were doing all those things. And he loves you even more now, because you've come to tell him you're sorry. He loves you just as you are, with all your sins, and not the ideal, perfect boy you'd like to be deep in your heart. Now, when you go back to your place in church, I want you, for your penance, to kneel down and ask God to bless all the people you've been mean to or hurt in any way. And then pray the Our Father for all of them together. Can you do that?"

"Yes, Father," he says.

"Good. Now listen while I give you God's forgiveness."

* * *

I hear confessions in a fine Catholic high school for boys. They come into church by classes for a brief Scripture reading and a talk by the school chaplain to help them prepare. They are free to go to a priest or not. Not all come. Some who do, however, move me deeply with their struggles: to reconcile with parents, siblings, and classmates; to try again to do their best at school when they've been lazy. The penance I most often give these boys starts with a question: "Do you think that before you go to bed tonight you could do something nice for one other person that would make that person feel happy?"

I can't remember ever being turned down. (If that happened, I would accept it at once and assign a devotional penance.)

"All right, then. Let's make it specific. Who are you going to do that for?" In nine cases out of ten, I hear: "My mom."

* * *

The voice on the other side of the confessional screen sounds tired, and discouraged.

"I just hope we've done enough, Father. Of course, the kids are grown up now, and only one of them still goes to Mass. But I just hope we've done enough."

"I don't know you," I respond. "And I don't know anything about your life. But if you ask me whether you've done enough, I have to tell you that you haven't done enough. How do I know that? Because *I* haven't done enough. The pope hasn't done enough. Even Mother Teresa didn't do enough. None of us has done enough. The Lord doesn't want you to worry about whether you've done enough. He wants you instead to put all your confidence and trust in the One who has done enough: Jesus Christ."

There is a long pause. Then, "Well, I've learned something today."

The rewards of priesthood, they say, are out of this world. Sometimes, however, God is very good and gives us a down payment.

* * *

I treasure the words of the late Tom Burns, longtime editor of the London *Tablet*:

> Those who have had the good fortune to travel widely and meet priests in many countries will agree that though they may have met embittered and frustrated men here and there, for the most part their encounter has been with dedicated men: unselfish to a degree, simple and honest and above all happy in their vocation. Such travelers must ask themselves if they can say the same of all their married friends.

Priests would give different reasons for this happiness. For me the supreme reason is the privilege, so far beyond any man's deserving, of offering daily the sacramental memorial of the one, full, perfect, and all-sufficient sacrifice of Calvary, and being nourished by—and distributing to the Lord's holy people—that daily bread for which Jesus taught us to pray.

* * *

"Have you ever regretted being a priest?" a young evangelical friend asked me.

"Never," I told him. "It's all I ever wanted."

31

My Replacement

The prophet Elijah, with Moses one of the two great Old Testament heroes who appeared with Jesus at his transfiguration, experienced his greatest triumph when he challenged the priests of the false god Baal atop Mount Carmel. The rules of the contest were simple. Each side would pray to its god. "And the god who answers by fire, he is God." The dramatic story is told in chapter 18 of the first book of Kings.

The following chapter 19 portrays Elijah's flight from the wicked king Ahab and his enraged queen Jezebel, who has vowed revenge. The Lord confronts the prophet, now in the depths of self-pity, in a cave near Mount Horeb.

"Why are you here, Elijah?"

"Because of my great zeal for the Lord of hosts."

We expect a paean of praise or at least a word of encouragement. God, as so often in Scripture, confounds our expectation. Instead of praising Elijah for his courage, God sends him to commission his replacement: "Go ... anoint Elisha son of Shaphat of Abel-meholah to be prophet in your place."

As I near the close of my eighth decade, I cannot know whether the years that remain to me will be many or few. What is certain is that no man is indispensable; Elijah's experience confirms this. It is time for me to be concerned about my replacement. What follows is for him.

* * *

Dear Stephen:

Though I have known you since you were three, you first came to my attention when you started serving at Mass at age eight or nine. Unlike the other boys (there were no girl servers then), you made all the responses and joined in the people's prayers. Your grandfather had tutored you. You are musical, so from an early age you sang in the choir. Later you started piano lessons and made such rapid progress that while you were still in high school you were able to substitute for our music director when he was away.

When you were entering high school, I invited you to dinner. Through questions, I led you to confirm what I already knew: you found the Church, and everything connected with it, fascinating.

"Stephen," I told you, "that's how the Lord calls us. He doesn't call us through a voice in the corner of the room. He calls us through circumstances. You should think about spending your life doing what you most enjoy, as a priest."

"I wouldn't be surprised if I ended up a priest," you told me.

You're in college now. Your interest in the Church has not

slackened. Your parents told me that when you were looking at colleges during your senior year in high school, at every college you visited, you enquired about the student chaplaincy. When I took you sailing in Maine last summer, with Michael and Paul, you participated with obvious devotion in our daily Mass on board. One afternoon, when the others had gone to get lobsters for our dinner, you and I had Mass together. You questioned me afterward about the priest's private prayers: at the preparation of the gifts and before Communion. Those were unusual questions for a young man of eighteen. They showed your continuing fascination with priesthood.

You're still not ready to commit. That is understandable. When Pope Benedict XVI submitted to a live television interview in August 2006 (for a pope, something unprecedented), he was asked about his message to youth. Here is some of what he said:

> Young people are very generous, but when they face the risk of a life-long commitment, be it to marriage or a priestly vocation, they are afraid... By making a definitive decision am I not forfeiting my personal freedom? I want to give young people the courage to make binding decisions: they are really the only ones that allow us to grow, to move ahead, and to reach something great in life. They are the only decisions that do not destroy our freedom but offer to point us in the right direction. Risk making this leap toward the definitive, I tell them, and so embrace life fully.[62]

"I like girls," you've told me. Thank God you do, Stephen. How can a man who has never known what it is to love, and be loved (and I'm talking about erotic love here), be truly what every priest is called to be, and what Jesus was and is: a man for others? When the Lord calls a man to priesthood, he is not asking him to give up love. He is asking him to surrender to a greater love, the love of the Lord himself. Only the man who has done that can bring this love to others.

"I'm not good enough," you say. Well of course you aren't! None of us is good enough to be a priest of the all-holy God: not the pope, not the holiest and best priest you know, certainly not myself. Paul knew that. "We have this treasure in earthen vessels," he wrote (2 Corinthians 4:7). God doesn't call us because we're good enough. He calls us because he loves us. And God does not call those who are fit, according to human reckoning. But he always fits those whom he calls.

If you have read the previous chapters of this book, you will know how unworthy of priesthood I was—and still am. If the Lord used me, he can use you. There are only two absolute disqualifications for priestly service. The Lord cannot use a man who will not work or cannot love. All other defects can be remedied, by his grace.

"I want to keep my options open," you say. Like most of your peers, you regard that as the key to happiness. It is not. The big rewards in life come to those who *choose* an option, and go for it, all out. Those who insist on keeping their options open are like butterflies, flitting from flower to flower. They skim over life's surface without ever plumbing its depths. They cheat themselves of all but the most passing rewards. Don't cheat yourself any longer, Stephen.

Do you pray? Of course you do. But is your prayer regular, consistent, disciplined? If you are still uncertain about your decision, prayer will clarify it. When you finally decide for priesthood, prayer is its indispensable foundation. The prayer I am talking about, however, must be more than a now-and-then thing. We can all pray when we feel like it. To be truly life changing and life supporting, prayer must be kept up when we *don't* feel like it.

If you have not yet done so, sit down with a trusted priest or other spiritual guide and draw up a rule of life for yourself. Set modest goals. Spending fifteen minutes in prayer faithfully five times a week for a full year is better than trying for a daily half hour and then giving up in a couple of weeks. The alpine guides in Switzerland can always spot the novice climbers. They start out too fast, soon tire, and fail to reach the summit. The experienced climber goes slowly, but reaches the goal. Think about that.

I won't tell you how to pray. There are many methods, and you should get help: from books, but also from a guide with experience of the spiritual journey. The only rule I know is: pray as you can, and not as you can't. But do it! You *must* spend time with the Lord: quality time, not just hasty minutes snatched from other activities or the last few minutes of the day when you are tired and can't concentrate.

Shared prayer with others is fine, if that helps you. And regular participation in the Church's public prayer is essential. But there is no substitute for spending time alone with the Lord. That is the only way to develop and deepen your friendship with him. And without a deep, personal friendship with Jesus Christ, no decision for priesthood can be sustained over a lifetime.

The Lord has given you a fine mind. Continue to develop

it. Turn off the TV and read. Reading stimulates the imagination. Television stultifies it. Anything that seizes your interest, fiction or nonfiction, is fine, provided that it is of good quality and not trash.

You will want to be the best preacher you can possibly be: a man excited about the message you have to deliver, able to communicate it with enthusiasm and to kindle this enthusiasm in others. You cannot acquire that ability through courses in public speaking. All the technical skills in the world will not make a man a good preacher if he has nothing to say. To remedy that defect (the root cause of almost all bad preaching), you must hit the books.

When you get to seminary, take your studies seriously. (Forgive me for jumping ahead here; that's how confident I am of your call.) Study is more important, frankly, than acquiring practical skills though what is these days called field education. Seminary is not the time to play priest. You have the rest of your life for that. It *is* the time to become professionally competent.

To be a professionally competent messenger and minister of Jesus Christ, you must have a good working knowledge of the great theological ideas of the Bible: God's progressive self-disclosure in history, election, grace, atonement, sin, repentance, forgiveness. Those ideas are exciting. People have fought and died for them. If you have never tasted that excitement yourself, how can you communicate it to others?

You'll need a good working knowledge of our doctrinal tradition, as the Church gives it to us ("the magisterium"). Before ordination you should have read enough moral theology to realize that many ethical questions are complex and not soluble simply by sanctified common sense. And you should know enough of our history to have discovered at least a few heroes and heroines who inspire you; and to realize that not all our problems are new.

Caring for the wonderful bodies the Lord has given us is just as important as care of the soul and mind. Continue your active interest in sports. Eat wholesome but not excessive meals. If you drink, be moderate and know when to stop. Make as many friends as you can, and be a good friend to others. But never fear solitude. You will spend much time alone as a priest. Prayer and reading will help you to find God in solitude.

Be prepared, finally, for discouragement, doubts, setbacks. One test of your vocation is the willingness to undergo these things and the drudgery that any vocation involves (and yes, that includes the vocation to marriage). I can promise you that it isn't all drudgery. I have not found it so. Neither will you. I cannot promise you glamour or riches or visible success. But I can promise you deep, abiding joy—the joy that comes from knowing that you are part of the greatest service in the world.

I know. I answered the Lord's call on my ordination day fifty-four years ago. I have never regretted it. Not one single day.

Your friend and brother, in Christ Jesus,
Fr. Jay Hughes

32

"When You Pray . . . "

When you pray, say, Our Father . . .

Luke 11:2

We do not even know how we ought to pray, but through our inarticulate groans the Spirit himself is pleading for us, and God who searches our inmost being knows what the Spirit means.

Romans 5:17

Rejoice always, never cease praying, render constant thanks.

1 Thessalonians 5:17

I love the Our Father. For lifelong Catholics it is a rote prayer, associated with the Rosary. For me it is the prayer I prayed so often in childhood, standing with my father and my sister and brother, by my mother's grave, never able to finish.

The "practice of the presence of God," begun as a twenty-year-old seminarian, has now become habitual, enriched by my mantra, *Maranatha*. During the day I find myself often repeating the syllables of that prayer-word, *Ma-ra-na-tha*, or the holy names, "Jesus, Mary, Joseph" with every step I take as I walk up or down stairs, down a hallway, from one room to another, back and forth to my car—with every breath and every heartbeat.

Although the wordless, imageless prayer of the mantra is my mainstay, there are also vocal prayers that have become dear to me through constant use. The Rosary, alas, is not one of them. Not that I haven't tried. I carry a small rosary with me at all times. But the only time I am able to pray it is when taking a walk or driving. I find it a rather mechanical kind of prayer, but better than not praying at all; meditating on the mysteries while saying the words is beyond me. Popularly ascribed to St. Dominic (1170–1221), the Rosary is actually older, but not much. Catholics went on quite happily without it for more than a thousand years. In this one respect I am content to be a first-millennium Catholic.

I love the *Anima Christ*. I always pray it in the silence after Communion:

> Soul of Christ, sanctify me
>
> Body of Christ, save me
>
> Blood of Christ, inebriate me
>
> Water from the side of Christ, wash me
>
> Passion of Christ, strengthen me
>
> O good Jesu, hear me
>
> Within thy wounds hide me

Suffer me never to be separated from thee

From the malicious enemy defend me

In the hour of my death call me

And bid me come to thee

That with thy saints I may praise thee

For all eternity. Amen.

From my father I learned another prayer that is especially fitting at the end of Mass. It comes, I believe, from an Eastern source.

> Grant, O Lord, that we who are your soldiers here may enjoy your peace hereafter; that the tongues which sing your praises may also speak the truth; that the feet which stand within your sanctuary may walk in the land of light; that we who look upon you in these sacred mysteries of your body and blood may one day behold you face to face, where you live and reign with your Father in the unity of the Holy Spirit, one God, forever and ever.
>
> Amen.

To St. Ignatius Loyola we owe the fine prayer:

> Teach us, good Lord, to serve you as you deserve:
> to give and not to count the cost;
> to fight and not to heed the wounds;
> to toil and not to ask for any reward,
> but that of knowing that we do your will.

The American *Book of Common Prayer* gives me the next prayer, based on Isaiah 30:15 and Psalm 46:10. I have modernized the Elizabethan English, which now strikes me as stilted.

> O God of peace, you have taught us by your prophet that in returning and rest we shall be saved, in quietness and confidence shall be our strength; lift us, we pray, by the indwelling of your Holy Spirit, to your presence, where we may be still and know that you are God, living and reigning with your Son Jesus in the unity of this same Spirit, now and forever.

The next prayer is from the same source, likewise modernized and expanded:

> O God, you have prepared for those who love you such good things as pass our understanding; pour into our hearts such love toward you, that we, loving you above all things, and in all things, may obtain your promises, which exceed all that we can desire.[63]

* * *

For my sixtieth birthday on May 14, 1988, I composed this litany of praise, thanksgiving, and repentance:

I praise you, Lord

> for my birth sixty years ago today.
>
> for my baptism and confirmation.
>
> for the sacrament of penance, through which you constantly forgive my sins.
>
> for the Eucharist, in which I receive your love, your power, your goodness, your joy, your peace.

for the gift of your Son, Jesus Christ, in all life's changes "the same, yesterday, today, yes and forever."

for your holy word, which enlightens and guides me on life's way.

for the gift of priesthood, which makes me the servant of your holy people, though unworthy, and the herald of your truth.

I thank you, Lord

for a wise upbringing at the hands of good and loving parents.

for a younger sister, brother, stepmother, and half-sister.

for loving friends to share my laughter, tears, struggles, triumphs, and defeats.

for a wonderful education, still unfinished.

for health, energy, and strength.

for fine food and "wine that makes glad the heart of man" (Psalm 104:15).

for music, the laughter of friends, and the joy of children.

for adventure, beauty, and romance—in many countries and on the ocean wave.

for deliverance from perils, known and unknown.

for hardships, rebuffs, humiliations, disappointments, failures, which remind me of my need of you.

for all who have inspired me, shamed me, reminded

me of my high calling as your son, your priest.

for the forgiveness of those I have wronged or disappointed.

for your boundless patience, reflected in the patience of fellow travelers on the pilgrimage to you.

Forgive me, Lord

for pride and arrogance and every evil way.

for stubbornness and insistence on my own will, my own ideas.

for words, looks, deeds that have inflicted pain.

for insensitivity to others' needs, weaknesses, and moods.

for seeking self instead of you.

for opportunities neglected, words of comfort never spoken, deeds of kindness left undone.

for bad examples given, confidences abused, promises unkept.

for yielding to discouragement, cynicism, and despair.

for seeking nourishment from idle dreams and neglecting today's achievements, satisfactions, and rewards.

Support me, Lord

all the day long, until the shadows lengthen, and the evening comes, and the busy world is hushed, and the fever of life is over, and my work is done. Then in your mercy grant me a safe lodging, a holy rest, and peace at the last.[64]

Stay with me, Lord

be my remaining journey long or short

stay with me; guide my vessel safely into port.

* * *

When I turned seventy, I started to pray daily that the years that remain to me would be fruitful. At the age of seventy-five I added a daily prayer for a happy and holy death. I am confident that both petitions will be answered. How, I gladly leave to the loving providence that has surrounded and upheld me all my life long.

* * *

I conclude with some words written in the face of his own death by one of the great men of the Church in his day, Cardinal Basil Hume, OSB, of Westminster:

> We each have a story, or part of one at any rate, about which we have never been able to speak to anyone. Fear of being misunderstood. Inability to understand. Ignorance of the darker side of our hidden lives, or even shame, make it very difficult for many people. Our true story is not told, or, only half of it is. What a relief it will be to whisper freely and fully into the merciful and compassionate ear of God. That is what God has always wanted. He waits for us to come home. He receives us, his prodigal children, with a loving embrace. In that embrace we start to tell him our story.

I now have no fear of death. I look forward to this friend leading me to a world where I shall know God and be known by Him as His beloved son.[65]

Endnotes

1 London: Hodder & Stoughton, 1971. In his later years Heenan was heard to say: "Anyone who wants to be a bishop today deserves to be made one." The remark helps to explain the title of his second volume, *A Crown of Thorns* (1974).

2 Joseph Ratzinger, *Glaube und Zukunft* (Munich: Kösel, 1970). pp. 124f.

3 J.R.Quinn, "The Strengths of Priests Today," in: *America* July 1, 2002, pp. 12–15, at 13.

4 Cited from Peter Seewald, *Benedikt XVI* (Berlin: Ullstein, 2005), p. 294.

5 Cited from Greeley's review of Dean R. Hoge, *The First Five Years of Priesthood*, in: *America,* Sept. 30, 2002.

6 Scenes from Christ's passion, normally affixed to the side walls of Catholic churches.

7 *Hamlet*, Act 4, scene ii.

8 J.J. Hughes, *Proclaiming the Good News: Homilies for the "C" Cycle* (Huntington, IN: Our Sunday Visitor, 1985) pp. 95f.

9 We never met. When I arrived at Kelham, I was told that McVeigh had left to become a Catholic. He died in 1997 as Abbot Bernard McVeigh of the Trappist Abbey in Lafayette, Oregon.

10 I am indebted to my Kelham contemporary, Richard Rutt, for these verses. They refer to subtle colors in the Kelham chapel invisible to me because of color-blindness. An Anglican bishop first in Korea and then in England, Richard Rutt is today a retired Catholic priest in the Plymouth diocese. George Every became a Catholic in 1972 and died in 2003 at the age of 94.

11 John Chapman, *Spiritual Letters* (London: Sheed & Ward, 1983, p. 104; original 1935).

12 See p. 182f. below.

13 Andrew Greeley, *The American Catholic: A Social Portrait* (New York: Basic Books, 1977); and *An Ugly Little Secret: Anti-Catholicism in North America* (Kansas City: Sheed, Andrew & McMeel, 1977).

14 *The Journal of Convention*, 1953, *Diocese of New York*, p. 92. I am grateful to Prof. William Franklin for providing this text. No women sat in the New York Convention of that era.

15 Sheridan Gilley, "The end of the Oxford Movement" in: *The Tablet* 18 March 1995.

16 The patronizing attitude toward women expressed in this remark would bear bitter fruit not many years later—and the end is not yet.

17 When I asked a visiting Russian Orthodox archbishop there what he thought about the Vatican Council recently announced by Pope John XXIII, he responded, "Why should we be interested in a foreign council?" What a long way we have come since then.

18 The "work of God," St. Benedict's name for the monastic office of psalms, readings, and prayers, which he calls the monk's principal work.

19 Rereading the journal of my 1959 pilgrimage, I discovered that he had taken me for a long walk in Rome when he was a student monk at San Anselmo. He became Abbot Primate and died in 1995. R.I.P.

20 A parish priest in Spain once took me for a member of Opus Dei. In Italy a Franciscan was sure I was a Jesuit. You win some and lose some.

21 Ian Ker, *John Henry Newman: A Biography* (Oxford: Clarendon Press, 1988) pp. 285 and 318.

22 Answering questions from priests in the northwestern Italian diocese of Aosta on 25 July 2005, Pope Benedict XVI said: "The pope is not an oracle; he is infallible on the rarest of occasions, as we know. Therefore, I share with you these questions, these problems. I also suffer." I could have used a little of this candor in 1959.

23 Cited from Henry St. John, *Essays in Christian Unity* (London: Blackfriars, 1955) p. 71.

24 J.H. Newman, *Apologia pro Vita Sua* (ed. David J. DeLaura; New York: W.W. Norton, 1968), 90f.

25 Contrary to a widespread belief among Catholic clergy, there is no question of Anglican clergy getting themselves "ordained over again" to resolve doubts about their orders. The participation of these prelates in the consecration of Anglican bishops is an expression of the intercommunion between the respective Church bodies. Such participation is reciprocal.

26 The sacraments of baptism, confirmation, and ordination confer what theologians call "indelible character" and hence cannot be repeated. If there is a doubt whether the sacrament in question has been received validly, it is administered conditionally. At conditional baptism, for instance, the minister says: "If you are not already baptized, I baptize you … "

27 Not so one of her co-Sisters, who said in shocked tones when I told her of my decision: "But Father, you have to deny everything." She was in my father's camp.

28 I went to considerable lengths to avoid publicity. I was becoming a Catholic *despite* what I had observed of American Catholicism. I did not want to add to Catholic complacency.

29 No funerals are permitted during the last three days of Holy Week.

30 Ian Ker, *John Henry Newman: A Biography* (Oxford: Clarendon Press, 1988)p. 320.

31 "It was an amazing system," a veteran of the pre-Vatican II American seminary system has commented. "For six years they dressed us like girls, treated us like children, and expected us to come out like men."

32 The examinations in Innsbruck, as still in the ecclesiastical universities in Rome, were oral to prevent cheating, which on an oral exam is impossible. It was assumed that students would cheat if they could.

33 The Ten Commandments appear twice in the Bible: in Exodus 20 and in Deuteronomy 5. In the Exodus version, which I learned as a child, the prohibition of adultery is number seven. This leaves me hopelessly confused when I encounter older Catholics (nuns especially) who confess their sins by number. I can never remember how the two versions differ.

34 "A woman's preaching is like a dog's walking on his hinder legs. It is not done well; but you are surprised to find it done at all" (Boswell, *Life of Johnson,* 31 July 1763.)

35 During my time there the diocese had some 2 million Catholics and 1,500 diocesan priests.

36 A shrewd woman to whom I related this dream years later commented: "You had chosen an antique religion. Your father was not confident it would support you."

37 "Bei Ratzinger fällt auch der stärkste Mann um," literally: "Before Ratzinger, falls even the strongest man over."

38 Their opinions have now been published in English translation: Christopher Hill and Edward Yarnold (eds.), *Anglican Orders: the Documents in the Debate* (Canterbury Press: Norwich, 1997). My own request for access to the documents, supported by Bishop Höffner, was denied.

39 J.J.Hughes, "Ministerial intention in the administration of the sacraments," *The Clergy Review,* 51 (1966) 763–776.

40 I recognized from the start that this was crucial. In my initial conversation with Joseph Ratzinger, I asked him: "What is the essence of ministerial priesthood?" His reply was a model of pedagogical wisdom: "You must find that out for yourself, Herr Hughes."

41 "*Ad condemnandos errores nostri temporis*": Denziger-Schönmetzer, *Enchiridion Symbolorum* (Freiburg: Herder, 1965) No. 1763.

42 Bévenot, "A Rescue for Anglican orders?" *Heythrop Journal*, July 1971, 297–300.

43 *The Tablet,* 20 May pp. 631–633, and 3 June 1995, pp. 698f.

44 G.H. Tavard, *A Review of Anglican Orders: The Problem and its Solution* (Collegeville/MN: M. Glazier/Liturgical Press, 1990) p. 148 n. 20 and p. 154 n. 1.

45 See p. 187f above.

46 I was dismayed when I saw the misunderstandings and oversimplifications in the *scriptum* of my lectures on the Reformation in Leuven. The American students who compiled it lacked the expertise of their German counterparts—a reflection of their inferior schooling, but also of their unfamiliarity with the magisterial tradition.

47 Loyola University Press, Chicago, 1990. It is tribute to the Society of Jesus that one of its university presses was allowed to publish this damning indictment.

48 The fact that my Catholic ordination in 1968 was conditional, allows me to date my priesthood from my 1954 ordination, the date listed after my name in the diocesan records in St. Louis, as previously in Münster.

49 J.J.Hughes, "The missing 'Last Words' of Gilbert Burnet in July 1687": *Historical Journal* 20 (1977) 221–227.

50 Our Sunday Visitor later published them in three volumes, under the title *Proclaiming the Good News.*

51 A favorite text, as alert readers will already have noted. The full text of the sermon was published in *The Priest* 36/1 (Jan. 1980), 40–43.

52 Legend relates that this St. John was thrown, bound and gagged, into the Moldau river in 1393 for refusing to tell the wicked and profligate King Wenceslaus IV what his blameless queen had said in confession.

53 A special privilege. American priests are normally paid by the parish or other institution that they serve.

54 John L. May, *With Staff and Pen* (Liguori Publications, Liguori, Mo.: 1992)

55 I owe this conclusion to Monsignor Kenneth Velo, who used it to conclude his magnificent funeral sermon for Cardinal Joseph Bernardin in Chicago on November 20, 1996. "Credit where credit is due" (a favorite saying of Bina's).

56 My father is in good company. In the Mexican cathedral of Puebla, the tomb of an archbishop has neither name nor dates, just the words: *Fideles, rogad por un pecador* ("Faithful, pray for a sinner.")

57 Roy Jenkins, *Gladstone* (Macmillan, London: 1995) p. 73.

58 An Aramaic word meaning "come, Lord." It derives from a first-generation Christian liturgy, where it was a prayer for Christ's return: (1 Corinthians 16:22b).

59 J.J.Hughes, *Centering Prayer: How to pray from the heart* (Liguori Publications, Liguori, Mo.: 1981)

60 At Marburg in 1529 Luther defended belief in the real presence against the Swiss Reformer Zwingli by writing in chalk on the table, "*hoc est enim corpus meum,*" and telling his opponent: "Take those words away, and I'll be content." Concern with an exact "moment of consecration," and its location in the words of institution were, however, late developments. For roughly the first millennium the

whole Eucharistic prayer was considered consecratory. See J.J.Hughes, *Stewards of the Lord*, pp. 179f.

61 *The Tablet*, 1 May 1993.

62 The interview was conducted in German. This is my translation of the official transcript.

63 How inferior, by contrast, is the rendering of this prayer in the Sacramentary: "God our Father, may we love you in all things and above all things and reach the joy you have prepared for us beyond all our imagining" (Twentieth Sunday in Ordinary Time.)

64 This prayer is composed from language used by Newman in two Anglican sermons from 1842 and 1843. I sometimes use it at burials and have asked that it be used at mine.

65 Cited from a homily preached by Monsignor (now Bishop) George Stack at a requiem Mass for the Cardinal in Westminster Cathedral on June 18, 1999.

Index